Career Handbook for Working Professionals

SECOND EDITION

Next Step Partners

Copyright © 2014 by Next Step Partners. All Rights Reserved

This publication is protected by copyright law. Reproduction in any form is strictly prohibited without the express permission of Next Step Partners.

ISBN: 978-0-9905535-0-2

Published by:
SF Press
San Francisco, CA

Book design and layout by Michelle Montbertrand

Second Edition
Printed in the USA

Introduction

Welcome! We are excited that you have chosen this handbook to help you take the next step in your career. Our work with thousands of professionals from all sectors across the U.S. and abroad has inspired its creation. We think you will find it a useful guide in managing your career, and the career transition process in particular.

The content and exercises in this handbook are intended to make this transition a more productive and rewarding experience, whether you are looking to change careers or are looking for a new position in your current field. Through this handbook, we will help you create focus and momentum around your goals while offering new frameworks, ideas and perspectives.

Whether you are unsure of your next move, are considering a few alternative paths, or are intently focused on a specific career, we encourage you to explore all that this handbook has to offer. We have organized the content to reflect the different phases of the job search process — starting with a Career Transition Roadmap, followed by Introspection and Self-Assessment, and continuing with Career Exploration and Job Search Execution. We have also included a section on Additional Resources to further assist you in your job search.

We welcome your thoughts and feedback for future editions of this handbook. Please email us at Info@NextStepPartners.com. We wish you great success as you take the next step in your career!

Next Step Partners

Table of Contents

PART 1 – CAREER TRANSITION ROADMAP — 1

Stages of Career Transition — 2
Staying Motivated — 4
Time Management — 9
Working with a Coach — 11
Types of Transitions — 12
    Fully Employed, Working Professionals — 12
    Part-time/Executive Degree Candidates — 13
    Unemployed Professionals — 14
    Professionals Re-entering the Workforce — 15
    Career Changers — 17
    Professionals Pursuing Entrepreneurial or Nontraditional Career Paths — 18
    Professionals Looking for Their Second Act — 19
    Happily Employed Professionals — 20

PART 2 – INTROSPECTION AND SELF-ASSESSMENT — 21

Outside Influences — 22
Values — 23
Vision — 31
Competencies — 35
Assessment Tools — 41
Mini-360 Assessment — 42
Describing Your Brand — 45

PART 3 – CAREER EXPLORATION — 49

The Exploration Process — 50
Experimentation — 52
Positioning Statement — 53
Networking — 56
Making Requests — 68
Cold and Warm Introductions — 70
Informational Interviews — 77
Action Planning — 83

Table of Contents

PART 4 – JOB SEARCH EXECUTION — 85

- Cover Letters — 86
- Resumes — 88
- Bios — 103
- Marketing Plan — 105
- Social Media — 110
- Working with Executive Recruiters — 113
- Exit Statement — 115
- Interview Preparation and Performance — 116
  - *Key Steps* — 116
  - *Company/Organization Research* — 119
  - *Types of Interview Questions* — 121
  - *Behavioral Interview Preparation* — 122
  - *Questions to be Ready for* — 129
  - *Phone/Video Interviews* — 131
  - *Interview Challenges* — 133
  - *Closing the Interview* — 137
  - *Thank-You Notes* — 138
- Job Search Productivity — 139
- Getting Unstuck — 140
- Managing Job References — 142
- Managing Timing of Offers — 144
- Evaluating Job Offers — 146
- Negotiation — 149

APPENDIX – ADDITIONAL RESOURCES — 159

- Values List — 160
- Action Verbs — 162
- Mock Interview Evaluation Form — 163
- Recommended Reading — 166
- Useful Websites — 169
- About Next Step Partners — 173

PART 1

Career Transition Roadmap

Stages of Career Transition

The career transition process, like any other life change, can be overwhelming, scary, challenging, and exciting. One moment we feel lost, and the next we are inspired by what seem like boundless opportunities that lie before us. Knowing more about the different, discrete stages of the career transition process that people may experience can help you address your current situation as well as anticipate what lies in store for you down the road.

THE FOUR STAGES

The first stage. The first stage in the career transition process is often one of shock, paralysis, or even denial. You face an unexpected situation that you don't want to be in. The situation may be triggered externally (*"I can't believe I got laid off!"*) or internally (*"I thought I would like being a lawyer, but I don't."*)

The second stage. In the second stage, you will experience some type of emotion about your situation, either positive or negative. You are accepting the reality of your situation, without quite knowing what to do about it. You might be feeling, *"I'm scared that I've been looking for months and I don't have a job yet."* Or the feeling might be one of elation, *"Woo hoo! I am glad to be done with my last job! Anything else will be better than that!"*

The third stage. The third stage of the career transition process involves exploring new possibilities. You feel excited about discovering new options, experimenting with new ideas, and meeting new people. You might think, *"I'm curious about what types of entrepreneurial ventures exist where I could apply my skills..."* or *"I wonder what it would be like to work in finance..."* or *"I'm eager to explore a new career path after taking time off..."*

The fourth stage. Finally, after much exploration, comes the fourth stage — commitment to a new path. There may still be uncertainties, but you are energized by your new direction and ready to move forward. You have a clear sense of how you fit in now, and how this new professional path and identity link to your previous ones. Here, you may say, *"After looking into several start-ups, I realized that I really like the resources and training that a large organization provides, along with a high-caliber peer group. This, combined with my interest in technology, has led me to focus on large software companies like Oracle, SAP, and Salesforce.com."*

Career development is cyclical. This means that it is inevitable that you will repeat the different stages of career transition over the years. This is how careers grow and develop.

Know where you are in this transition process. If possible, we recommend that you *not* interview for jobs while you are in the first and second stages, which can be very emotionally charged. These emotions are likely to show through in your communications with others, whether or not you think you are doing a good job of hiding them, and may result in less-than-desired outcomes. More importantly, your emotions in the early stages — whatever they may be — are valid and need to be fully experienced for you to move on to the third stage where you can explore options more productively.

The chart on the following page illustrates this four-stage career transition process.

Stages of Career Transition

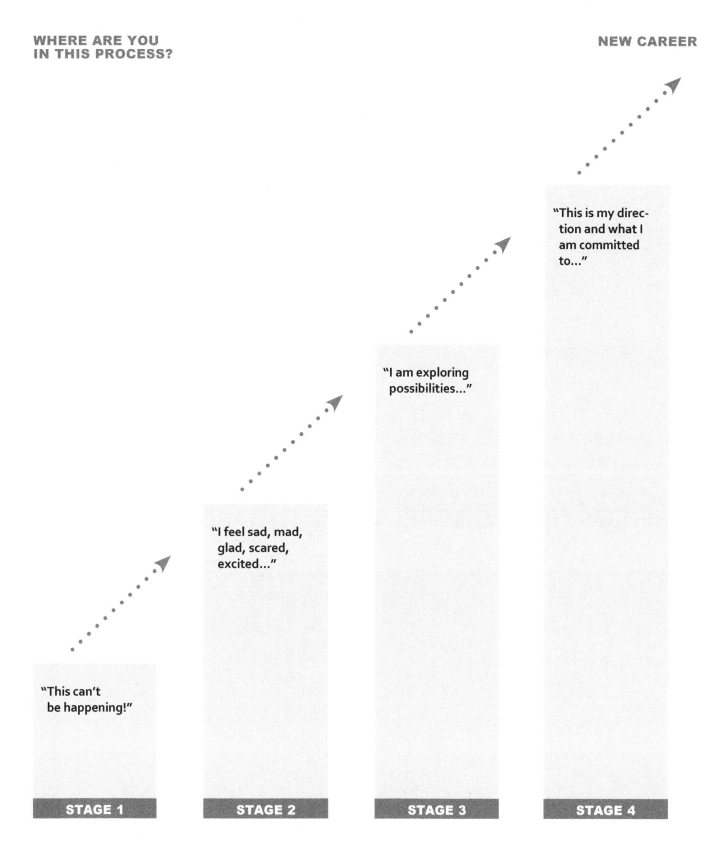

Staying Motivated

Career transition is often a stressful time. Finding your next position can take from just a few weeks to several months or more. As a result, it is important to stay motivated. Motivation comes from staying energized, building personal resilience, setting effective goals, and being held accountable to those goals.

STAYING ENERGIZED

Make sure that your days include activities that energize and revitalize you. This will help your overall sense of well-being and your performance in the networking and interviewing process. Your mood and energy level (or lack thereof) will show in your interactions with others and can influence your success in the career transition process.

ENERGIZING ACTIVITIES

List below 15 activities that you really enjoy and that energize you.

Examples: Working out; Listening to music

1.
2.
3.
4.
5.
6.
7.
8.
9.
10.
11.
12.
13.
14.
15.

ACTION PLAN

Choose three activities from the list above that you will commit to doing in the next week.

Activity	How Often	When	With Whom
1.			
2.			
3.			

Staying Motivated

BUILDING RESILIENCE

Resilience is a key part of navigating the career transition process and the job search. There will be days when you are quite productive — people are responding to your requests, interviews are being scheduled, and you are making good progress. On other days, things will seem to be at a standstill. You've sent several emails, yet there has been no reply. You feel lost, frustrated, and stuck.

This slowdown and uncertainty can shake your confidence. An effective way to reinforce or strengthen your resilience when you need it most is to draw upon past challenges that you have overcome.

DRAWING UPON PAST CHALLENGES

Note an experience that was stressful, difficult, or challenging in some way and how you handled this experience effectively.

How did this experience make you feel?

What characteristics or behaviors did you demonstrate that got you through this difficult time?

What do you know about yourself based on this experience?

Given your answers above, how can you apply this knowledge to your current situation?

We can also learn from others' experiences in handling challenge or adversity to inspire us and build our resilience. Which people do you admire for their resilience?

Staying Motivated

GOAL SETTING & ACCOUNTABILITY

Setting goals is another way to stay motivated. Goals need to be *specific* and *realistic* to be effective in helping us accomplish what we want. Below are some examples of less effective and more effective goals:

EXAMPLE 1	*Less effective:*	Talk to people in Biotech
	More effective:	Talk to three people this week who currently work or used to work in Biotech
EXAMPLE 2	*Less effective:*	Get a job in Biotech
	More effective:	Obtain three interviews this month in Biotech
EXAMPLE 3	*Less effective:*	Exercise more
	More effective:	Run for 30 minutes, twice a week

Example 1 addresses a natural tendency we have to be vague. Keeping goals vague allows too much wiggle room in how well we perform against our goals. We are not held as accountable for the results. The more specific goal of talking to three people in a week allows us to measure our performance concretely against the goal and better describes precisely the type of people we want to talk with.

While the less effective goal of *"Getting a job in Biotech"* in **Example 2** illustrates aiming high, which we certainly encourage people to do, it does little or nothing in terms of indicating what we need to do *right now*. Being clear about the interim steps toward achieving the goal better directs our efforts.

Like Example 1, **Example 3** shows the difference between a vague goal and a specific goal. Often, we speak in terms of "more" or "less." What does more or less mean for *you*? Clarifying this makes the goal more likely to be achieved.

For goals to keep us motivated, we need to be held accountable — either to ourselves or to others, or both. If you are good at holding yourself accountable to your goals — bravo! If you need help in this area, ask a friend or colleague to hold you accountable. Ask your accountability partner(s) to do the following:

- Ask you for clarification/specificity when goals you set are unclear or vague
- Challenge you to do more than you originally considered
- Ask you what got in the way if you did not achieve a particular goal in the time specified
- Applaud you when you do what you said you would do and ask, *"Was that too easy for you? What would be more of a challenge?"*
- Help you to set your next goal(s)

Each goal you set should answer:

- *What* will be done?
- By *when*?
- How will my accountability partner know when it is done?

This last part — how my accountability partner will know when it is done — is the accountability structure that you establish together. Will you talk by phone, email each other, or meet in person? And how often? Daily, weekly, biweekly? This check-in, or feedback loop, helps strengthen the accountability.

Staying Motivated

MOMENTUM MATRIX

The *Momentum Matrix* is a tool for you to use, either on your own (if you are good at holding yourself accountable) or with your accountability partner(s). We recommend weekly check-ins to keep the momentum going. We encourage you to set goals related to your career transition and job search, as well as more personal goals, since these help you to maintain your energy and well-being. Thus, you might include items from the list of energizing activities on *page 4*.

In each check-in or accountability meeting, the following questions should be asked and answered for each person:

- What did you say you were going to do?
- What did you actually do?
- What will you do for next week?

	GOAL	ACTUAL
EXAMPLES	• Call 5 existing real estate contacts • Join at least 2 real estate groups on LinkedIn • Attend 2 networking events • Conduct 2 informational interviews • Run 3 times this week for 1 hour • Attend 1 cultural event	• Called 7 existing contacts • Joined 3 real estate groups on LinkedIn • Attended 1 networking event • Asked for 3 informational interviews, conducted 1 • Ran M, T, W, F • Went to photography exhibit
WEEK OF _____		
WEEK OF _____		
WEEK OF _____		
WEEK OF _____		

©2014 Next Step Partners | www.NextStepPartners.com

Staying Motivated

MOMENTUM MATRIX

	GOAL	ACTUAL
WEEK OF _____		
WEEK OF _____		
WEEK OF _____		
WEEK OF _____		
WEEK OF _____		
WEEK OF _____		

Time Management

One of the biggest obstacles working professionals face in making proactive career changes is time. It takes time to find a job, and it takes time to figure out what you really want. The problem of time is not unique; everyone faces time constraints in one form or another. If you are delaying starting your job search until you have enough time, you will probably be waiting a long time.

Being successful in your career transition requires you to do two things: (1) make your career exploration a priority, so that it doesn't always slip to the bottom of the pile; and (2) adopt time-management techniques that are going to work for you.

Slow and steady wins the race

A solid career search can easily take scores of hours over a period of months. In general, you are better off spending a small, fixed period of time on your search every day rather than planning on bursts of sustained activity at irregular intervals. There are several reasons for this:

- It may take days or weeks for people to respond to your emails or phone calls; when responses do come, they tend to trickle in.
- Your energy and enthusiasm will vacillate throughout the process; if you only work on your search when you feel motivated, you may have many down periods.
- Spending a long period of time on certain tasks, such as internet research, can lead to diminishing returns; it may be difficult to pull yourself out of activities that are not fruitful.
- By making your search a daily part of your life, however brief, you are making it a habit; you will be subconsciously attending to your search throughout the day, rather than abandoning it for days or weeks at a time. Even if you do one small thing a day, you will be making progress.
- Putting off major tasks — like rewriting your resume or updating your LinkedIn profile — may make the tasks seem bigger and scarier than they really are. There's a lot of value in constant, small improvements.
- If you are doing a search that requires much networking, it typically takes several weeks, or even months, of planting seeds before things begin to sprout. If you only work on your job search sporadically, it's much harder to get this momentum going.

FINDING TIME

There are several techniques you can use to find time where none appears to be available.

- Start work half an hour early, so that you have a quiet period early in the day to research, send emails, or make phone calls.
- Meet networking contacts for breakfast or lunch on a regular basis; two or three meetings per week will create good momentum in your job search.
- Consider setting up phone meetings rather than in-person meetings if you are very pressed for time or travel frequently.
- Conduct a quick audit of your own time-wasting activities (e.g., reading blogs, internet surfing or computer games, aimless chatter with colleagues, etc.) and commit to substituting meaningful job-search exploration for one of these.
- Instead of setting "minimum" times for working on projects (such as editing your resume), set "maximum" times. For example, instead of declaring, "*I have to work on my resume for at least two hours this weekend,*" try "*I'm going to work on my resume for 45 minutes at lunch and not a minute more.*"

Time Management

ASSESS ACTUAL TIME REQUIREMENTS

Time management is a lot easier when you have an idea of how long things actually take.

Exercise:

Make a list of at least 10 job-search activities you anticipate undertaking. Estimate how much time they will actually require. This list can be a direct guide in helping you to figure out how to spend your time, particularly small increments of time, that might otherwise be wasted.

ACTIVITY	TIME REQUIRED
Examples:	
Contact former boss to get input on my search	10 min to set up, 1 hour for talk
Rewrite resume	2–3 hours
Search LinkedIn for contacts in digital media	15 minutes

1.
2.
3.
4.
5.
6.
7.
8.
9.
10.

PLAN AHEAD

Another method to help you manage your time effectively is to do the following:

- On Sunday evening, look at your calendar for the upcoming week and assess how much time you can commit to your search that week. Ask yourself, "*What will I need to have accomplished toward my job search by Friday afternoon so that I will feel that I've been productive this week?*" Given your answer to this question, what do you need to do each day? Working backward like this can put the wheels in motion to make things happen by the end of the week.

- Every evening, look at your calendar to determine what you can do the following day. If you don't look at your calendar until the next day, half the day will be gone before you get around to focusing on your job search and there may be little you can accomplish for that day. There are many small, but important, activities you can accomplish with just a little foresight.

SCHEDULE TIME

Scheduling time on your calendar for job search activities can help to create the discipline that may otherwise be lacking. Just as you might schedule an appointment with a personal trainer at the gym, or time to see a movie with a friend, make an appointment with yourself to spend time on your job search activities. Be realistic about the time that you can commit and disciplined about keeping the time you set aside.

Working with a Coach

NEXT STEP PARTNERS

WHAT IS COACHING?	Coaching is a rapidly growing field that has gained wide recognition as an effective way to help individuals achieve greater performance and satisfaction in their personal and professional lives. Much like a sports coach, a career or executive coach can help you to attain better results.
WHY WORK WITH A COACH?	Working with a coach can help you to articulate your goals and map out the milestones toward achieving these goals, no matter how high they may be. In mapping out these milestones, a coach will help you determine the actions required to achieve results and will hold you accountable. A coach will also assist you in clarifying any obstacles (both real and perceived) to reaching your goals. By assisting you to clarify obstacles, a coach can help you overcome or bypass these obstacles, thereby making your goals more attainable. Coaching can also help you to: • Learn new skills • Make better decisions • Focus on what you really want and enjoy • Aim higher and achieve more • Take more control • Reduce stress • Feel more fulfilled
WHAT SHOULD YOU EXPECT FROM A COACH?	You should expect total confidentiality and a safe, nonjudgmental environment in which to express yourself. In a coaching relationship, you should expect your coach to listen more than talk. Your coach should be honest and direct with her observations, while still encouraging and supportive of your goals.
HOW DOES COACHING DIFFER FROM CONSULTING?	Coaching is a process by which the coach helps *you* find the answers, while consulting involves providing the solutions. Coaching focuses on taking action to get results.
WHAT TO LOOK FOR IN A COACH	When looking to hire a coach, you should inquire about the individual's professional background and where he has received his coaching training and certification. While coaching is not currently a licensed profession, you still want someone who has received formal training in the field. It can be helpful, but is not necessary, if the coach also understands your background or industry. What is most important when selecting a coach, is that he or she is an expert in guiding individuals through a career transition, or other stages of career development, and that you feel this person would best support you through the process you are about to undertake.
HOW TO FIND A COACH	If you are in a degree program, your university may provide access to coaching staff at the Career Center. Likewise, your undergraduate or graduate schools may have an alumni career staff person available to meet with you for short-term coaching. However, for longer-term coaching, the career center may refer you to a professional coach who is available for assistance on a more regular basis. Check with your schools for a list of prescreened and qualified coaches. You can also ask friends for referrals (just as you would for any other service provider), or consult the International Coach Federation website at *www.coachfederation.org*.

Types of Transitions

CAREER TRANSITION PATHS

There are many different types of career transition, depending on your individual situation. You may find that you fall into more than one of the categories below.

- Fully Employed, Working Professionals
- Part-time/Executive Degree Candidates
- Unemployed Professionals
- Professionals Re-entering the Workforce
- Career Changers
- Professionals Pursuing Entrepreneurial or Nontraditional Career Paths
- Professionals Looking for Their Second Act

Your personal situation, however unique, will determine some of the specific issues that you face and the topics that are most important for making a successful transition.

FULLY EMPLOYED, WORKING PROFESSIONALS

By "Working Professionals," we mean people who have been working for some time, are currently employed, and are not currently in school, yet are contemplating a career transition. If this describes you, you'll want to address some key areas.

Create space for reflection

When you have been working for a number of years in a particular field, the easiest job to get is likely to be similar to your current job, or a natural extension of it. But the easiest path is not necessarily the right path for you. When looking for a new opportunity, take time to make sure it is the *right* opportunity. You don't want to land a new job to find that it is just more of the same. Take a step back and ask, "*What do I really want?*" For individuals with extremely consuming jobs, stepping back may require taking a break — perhaps a vacation, a leave of absence, or, if necessary, even leaving the position altogether.

Update your sense of what you bring to the table

If it's been many years since you last looked for a job, you may have a slightly outdated sense of your competencies. Alternatively, your competencies may include useful skills, knowledge, and traits not required by your current job, so be ready to articulate these, if appropriate. (*See pages 35–40 for ways to articulate your competencies.*)

Be diligent about time management

Looking for a job takes a lot of time, something that working professionals do not have in abundance. Taking just 10–15 minutes a day to do the small, yet important, tasks involved in a career transition can be fruitful and create the necessary momentum to get a job search going. (*See pages 9–10 for further time management tips.*)

Avoid the "I've Never Had to Look for a Job" Trap

Some people have gotten all of their previous jobs with minimal effort because their jobs have just "fallen into their lap" — perhaps through referrals, mentors, or on-campus recruiting. If this describes your career progression to date, be aware that many careers have veered off-course in this way. Proactively think about how you want your career to evolve, and intentionally go after what you want. Moreover, just because jobs fell into your lap before doesn't mean they will now.

Types of Transitions

PART-TIME/ EXECUTIVE DEGREE CANDIDATES

If you are working full-time and going to school part-time, you may face particular challenges, many of which relate to the logistical difficulties of mounting a major search effort while you are handling all of your other work and personal responsibilities. To be successful in your career transition or job search, put the following tips into practice:

Make your job search a priority

Although it's likely that the combination of full-time work, part-time school, and personal responsibilities is already very weighty, the fact is that you cannot let your job search take a back seat to your other duties. You will need to carve out time at regular intervals to do research, as well as network and interview.

Don't expect your credentials to sell themselves

Participants in part-time and executive degree programs often believe that they will receive more job offers with better potential salaries than students in full-time programs because they continue to gain work experience even as they are earning additional degrees. This is only likely to happen if you can specifically articulate to employers what your value is. Further, your job search is likely to be an independent search, as opposed to being focused on companies that recruit on-campus, so you will need to take a proactive approach.

Differentiate yourself

A good approach to making yourself stand out to employers is to highlight the unique ways that your work and academic pursuits have complemented each other. Talk confidently about how you've managed your work, school, and personal responsibilities — it says a lot about how you'll be able to achieve success on the job.

Build and activate your network

Individuals in part-time programs probably have the greatest potential networks of any category of job-seeker, since they retain access to their existing networks and have the opportunity to create new ones, starting with classmates in their part-time or executive program. However, it is up to you to put in the effort to make these *potential* benefits from networking real ones. Even if you plan to stay with your employer for the foreseeable future, invest time in developing your network — it will pay off in years to come, whether you stay at the same company or decide to pursue new opportunities.

Be clear about your obligations to your employer

If your current employer is sponsoring you in a part-time, executive, or other professional program, be familiar with your contractual responsibilities (e.g., are you financially responsible for the cost of your program if you take a new job within a specified period of time?).

Types of Transitions

UNEMPLOYED PROFESSIONALS

All other things being equal, most people would prefer to still have a job while looking for their next job for reasons of financial security, as well as for a *perceived* stronger negotiating position with potential employers. However, being unemployed is not the kiss of death that many people think. If you are conducting a job search and are unemployed, keep the following in mind.

Focus on your competencies

Your competencies are what you bring to the table. You will be in a stronger position if you focus on these rather than starting each meeting with an explanation of why you're not working. *See pages 35–40* to help you articulate your competencies.

Create a solid exit statement

Be able to describe in an honest but concise way why you are not working or why you left your last position. Then refocus the conversation on your qualifications and the potential opportunity.... When it comes to these statements, shorter is better. For example:

> *"I loved my six years at my last company. I had a once-in-a-lifetime opportunity to work as a humanitarian aid volunteer for six months — a cause that means a lot to me — so I took it. Now that I've completed that project, I'm ready to explore my next opportunity!"*

> *"We had a merger and there were several rounds of layoffs — I was ultimately part of the 10% of the workforce that was let go. Since we're in the same industry, I've always been familiar with your firm. Given my previous role, I'm confident that I could make an immediate contribution at your firm."*

See *page 115* for more on *Exit Statements*.

Don't present yourself as a victim

Generally speaking, people like to be around winners. A winner can be someone who's had great successes or it can be someone who has been resilient and has dealt well with the situations he or she has experienced. If you have experienced a negative episode in your career, think about what you've learned or gained from the experience, and practice talking about that.

> *"The last three months of our start-up were quite a tumultuous period, but I learned a huge amount about how to deal with high-pressure situations, keep my team's morale up, and manage the Board."*

> *"There are few openings in this industry, but I've developed some great leads and I feel good about how my search is going."*

Establish your bottom line

Being unemployed while looking for a job will only put you in a weaker position *if you let it!* You can signal to potential employers that despite not being employed at the moment, you expect to be paid a competitive salary. You can (and should!) do this in a way that does not come across as arrogant or entitled. For example, conveying that you are willing to be patient for the right opportunity signals to the employer that you are not desperate to take the first low-ball offer that comes along. We have seen many of our unemployed clients turn down offers that were below market rates or were unappealing in some other way. In these cases, they viewed their next-best alternative — which was having time to look for a better opportunity with better pay — as more valuable than the offer presented to them. We recognize that this is not always easy — it takes practice.

Types of Transitions

PROFESSIONALS RE-ENTERING THE WORKFORCE

There are many reasons for leaving the workforce. We are most aware of parents who leave the workforce to care for children, but many other reasons cause people to depart traditional employment. An individual may wish to care for a sick relative or aging parents, reconsider career options, travel, work on a nontraditional or creative project, explore starting a business, and so forth.

While the stories for leaving the workforce are different, the issues of re-entry are similar. Basically, you need to get the potential employer to focus on what you can immediately bring to the table and how you expect to grow going forward.

All of the tips that apply to those in the unemployed category on the previous page, apply here as well: focus on your competencies, have a solid exit statement, don't present yourself a victim, and have a bottom line. In addition:

Actively learn

If you have not worked for several years, you may not be up to speed on the latest trends, buzz words, and market dynamics. Read relevant news sources like the *New York Times* and the *Wall Street Journal*, as well as relevant blogs, and set up informational interviews with the people who are doing what you are interested in doing. Take advantage of on-line resources, read books, take courses, and go to conferences to show your passion and commitment. Update your understanding of the sector you seek to enter (or re-enter) and have a strong sense of how your interests and skills support the market needs.

Get back in touch with your competencies

Many people who have taken time out from their careers feel diminished self-confidence in what they can do or how they can contribute to an employer — regardless of how impressive their past accomplishments may have been! Engaging in activities, such as volunteering or taking on individual projects, can build your confidence by putting your best talents to use. (*See pages 35–40* to objectively review your accomplishments, both personal and professional.) The better you feel about yourself and your potential contribution to an employer, the more you will inspire confidence from other people and the more effective you will be in your search.

Aim for good growth opportunities, not immediate validation

Don't obsess about matching your last professional job, either in salary or in title. Employers may apply a discount factor to your experience the longer you've been between jobs. Instead of looking for immediate validation, look for opportunities where you can create something great going forward.

Look beyond executive recruiters

Executive recruiters, especially external ones, are generally looking for easy matches (*see pages 113–114* on *Working with Executive Recruiters*). Focus on creating situations where people can meet you in person and understand the value you bring — so spend ample time on networking.

Go offline

Online searches or want ads are unlikely to yield promising leads. People often spend countless hours doing online searches, to their great frustration, because each online search seems easier than networking. You will be much better off developing and leveraging your personal and professional contacts.

For a sample career re-entry resume, *see pages 99–100*.

Types of Transitions

PROFESSIONALS RE-ENTERING THE WORKFORCE

Observe where you get positive feedback

Career change often involves changing identities. If you are re-entering the workforce after several years, the people who know you best may not be the ones who give you the best reinforcement for rejoining the workforce. Hang out with people who are constructive, know your professional capabilities, and are supportive of your desire to start working again.

Get other support

Re-entering the workforce can be scary. It's like merging onto a fast-moving freeway. Be sure to have a solid support system during this time. Whether it is working with a coach or meeting regularly with others who are also trying to re-enter the job market, having the support from others can keep you inspired, confident, and moving forward in your job search.

Ease your way in

One possible way to make the transition back into the workforce is to start gradually. Rather than going from zero to 60 in a flash, look for part-time or temporary positions, or independent consulting projects, to get you acclimated to the work environment. It's also a good way to test out a new employer to see if it is a good fit, as well as see how deeply you want to dive in later.

Practice interviewing

How you communicate makes a huge difference. Practice what you say in interviews and networking situations with a variety of people and ask for direct feedback. Most job hunters have no idea how much they could improve their communication. A few hours of practice can dramatically improve your performance. (*See pages 116–138* on *Interview Preparation and Performance*.)

Types of Transitions

CAREER CHANGERS

Whether you are looking to make a slight shift in your career direction, or want to effect a more dramatic career change, consider the following:

Be willing to make an investment in a new direction

It's unusual to make a direct lateral or upward move when you switch careers. (In other words, mid-level attorneys rarely immediately become mid-level screenwriters). It's more likely that your first job in a new career will be a lower step onto a different ladder. If you are capable and experienced, in all likelihood you will progress quickly. This investment may be the proverbial one step back to take two steps forward, or it may be an actual investment in training or education that will position you to make your desired career change. Either way, this investment will clearly demonstrate to potential employers that you are committed to this new direction and they will be more inclined to take you seriously.

Make your network consistent with your career goals

Changing careers often means changing your professional identity, and that can require changing your immediate circle of contacts to include people who were not previously part of your network. Hang out and associate with people you want to be like, not the ones you are most comfortable with. (*See pages 56–67* for the section on *Networking* to assess your current network and create an action plan that is consistent with your career goals.)

Be ready to articulate your transferable competencies

Understand the top five competencies required for your desired career and be able to describe yourself and your experience in those terms. Show employers how your competencies are completely transferable to the job for which you are interviewing (even if they never ask you directly!). Doing so will reduce your perceived risk as a candidate in the employer's eyes. (*See pages 35–40* to articulate your competencies.)

Accentuate the positives of your past experience while focusing on the future

Talking about how your last career was boring or a mismatch is not very enticing to your potential employer. Cull some positives from your last experience, describe them, and then talk about how you'd like to build your career going forward. For example, *"My career as a CPA allowed me to interact with clients at a senior level, which I enjoyed very much. I am now looking to apply my analytical skills to a more creative endeavor, while still putting my client skills to use."* (*See page 115* for more examples of *Exit Statements*.)

Avoid ego-based phrases

Certain phrases, like *"I'm too senior,"* *"I'm too expensive,"* or *"I've already paid my dues"* suggest both a sense of entitlement and a sense of insecurity. Delete these from your vocabulary.

Types of Transitions

PROFESSIONALS PURSUING ENTREPRENEURIAL/ NONTRADITIONAL CAREER PATHS

If you are planning to pursue an entrepreneurial or nontraditional employment path, are the content and exercises of this handbook relevant to your search? Absolutely! If you are on the road less traveled, it's all the more important that you understand yourself, communicate what you offer, and create what you want. Keep in mind that the road less traveled is becoming increasingly crowded. Writer Dan Pink estimates in his book, *Free Agent Nation*, that nearly one-quarter of the U.S. workforce is either self-employed or working in entrepreneurial endeavors. This figure is estimated to hit 40% by 2020, according to a study conducted by Intuit.

Develop specific hypotheses of what you'd like to do

Many would-be entrepreneurs are more interested in the idea of starting and running an independent enterprise than in a specific type of business. However, if you speak too generally — "*I want to work for a start-up*" or "*I want to be involved in something I'm passionate about*" — it will be difficult for people to help you. Create a few hypotheses of the types of opportunities you might like to pursue. Use examples of known entities to trigger thinking.

> "*I'm looking for opportunities in start-ups. I have a specific interest in enterprises that offer new technologies over the web — early-stage versions of companies like Skype or WebEx would be ideal!*"

> "*I'm interested in working on the issue of childhood obesity. Some possible avenues might be working in a community-based organization, such as an organization that runs sports or nutritional programs for kids, or in a larger foundation that works on this issue, such as the Clinton Foundation.*"

> "*I'm considering creating a home-based business. Two ideas I'm thinking about are a concierge service and a child-care referral service. I'd love to speak with people who have worked in service businesses to flesh out some of my ideas.*"

Know your competencies

All organizations need people who can get the job done, but entrepreneurial ventures are even more focused on what you bring to the table rather than where you came from. Emphasize the skills, knowledge and traits that you offer, rather than your employment chronology. If you are unclear about the competencies required for your past jobs, ask yourself, "*If I had to hire someone to do exactly what I did in the past, what competencies would that person need to have?*" See pages 35–40 for more on *Competencies*.

Consider how you fit on the team

If you are thinking of launching your own enterprise, don't just hire people who are like you. Instead, think about what your own best contribution is, and what additional elements others can bring, or how they can complement you. "*I'm good at strategy and moving things forward, but I need someone who can do finance and accounting, someone who is strong at sales, and someone who can run all the IT.*" Similarly, if you are trying to join an entrepreneurial effort, analyze how your own competencies will complement those of the existing team and market yourself on that basis.

Be flexible about entry points

If you are very senior, you may not find a title and salary commensurate with your most recent traditional job. Don't let that distract you. Focus on how the upward trajectory looks, rather than your initial entry point.

Types of Transitions

PROFESSIONALS PURSUING ENTREPRENEURIAL/ NONTRADITIONAL CAREER PATHS

Do due diligence!

New enterprises, including social ventures and sole proprietorships, present a multitude of unknowns. Avoid the temptation to jump into the first thing that sounds exciting. Do your due diligence. This may include evaluating the business plan, investigating funding sources, checking out the competition, speaking with the board or other stakeholders, getting to know your future colleagues, and ironing out what would be expected of you in the next 90 to 180 days. Minimize risk while still connecting you to opportunities by doing project work or serving as an advisor. These roles allow you to get in the door, establish credibility, and scope out the most suitable role.

PROFESSIONALS LOOKING FOR THEIR SECOND ACT

If you are approaching retirement but aren't quite ready to retire and are thinking about what's next in your career and you are reading this handbook, you are likely wondering what specifically you want to do in your "second act," and how you are going to make it happen! That's good thinking, and many of the exercises in this handbook will help you.

Focus on engagement, not leisure

As the research psychologist Mihaly Csikszentmihalyi has shown in his book, *Finding Flow*, fulfillment does not come from leisure, it comes from *engagement*. Your form of engagement may come from starting another career, or it may come from working in your garden, improving your golf game, or having a reduced schedule/spending more time with family. But it's not going to come from having nothing to do.

Clarify values

Now that you're really a grown-up, ask yourself who you really are, and in particular, who you are *now*. As you contemplate your future options, you have the chance to make them align with your authentic values more than ever before. Use the exercises in this handbook to analyze what your values really are. These can be found on *pages 23–30*. Read some of the books recommended at the end of this handbook — they are some of the best guides to really understanding yourself and the process of creating the next version of you.

Create structure

Time and freedom feel great, until they don't feel great anymore. Impose the degree of structure that works best for you. This may include part-time work, volunteer activities, exercise routines, scheduled trips — whatever regimens make you feel *"on."*

Maintain and access your network

There are several reasons to put real energy into maintaining and accessing your network.

First, if you depart from a traditional work environment, you will probably not naturally access as many people as you normally would, and you may feel a significant absence of human connection.

Second, your network will be the best source of opportunities for you, whether those are for work, community involvement, or fun. Third, if a second-act career is a chance for you to be a new person, then accessing your network and experimenting with different types of positioning statements will be a great way to help develop this new identity. (See *pages 53–55* and *pages 56–67* on *Positioning Statements* and *Networking*, respectively).

For a sample second-act resume, *see pages 101–102*.

Types of Transitions

HAPPILY EMPLOYED PROFESSIONALS

If you have no intention of leaving your current job but are nonetheless reading this handbook — we congratulate you! You are doing the right thing. You can use this handbook to support your long-term career growth as well as lay the groundwork for your next job.

Build your network

A theme of this handbook is *"network, network, network."* Other people are critical to our long-term career success and satisfaction. They provide information, opportunities and — let's not forget — meaningful human interaction. So take the time to revisit existing ties and develop new ones. Examine the kind of network you should have, given your career goals, and create a strategy to achieve that.

Assess competency gaps

The competencies required to succeed in a given career path change over time. Analyze the competencies that will be required in your desired career five years into the future. Create a plan for developing them. This may include taking on new projects, completing a job rotation, taking courses and so on.

Communicate your interests and goals

The positioning statement is crucial even if you're not looking for a job. That's because it's your core message about what's important to you, what you seek to achieve, and how you want to grow. You're putting some kind of message out into the world — make sure it's one that serves you.

Understand your values as a key to work/life balance

Work/life balance isn't really about time management. Instead, it's about being able to express the values that are important to you, both in work and in life. Get clear about your values, and analyze how sufficiently they are currently expressed in your life.

Learn and experiment

Experimentation is the way we examine new possibilities, and you don't have to quit your existing job to find ways to experiment with alternatives. Consider new projects, volunteer activities, advisory roles, task forces, reading on topics that interest you, and informational interviews. If you are an expert in certain areas, let yourself be a beginner in other areas — being a neophyte can be liberating!

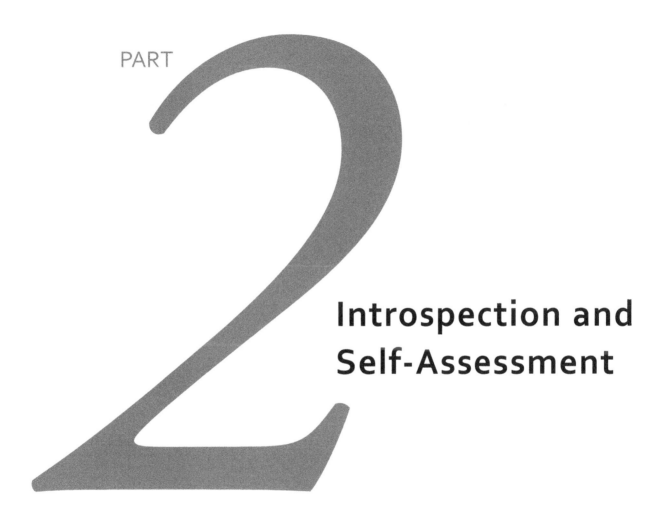

PART 2

Introspection and Self-Assessment

Outside Influences

We receive and internalize a lot of messages from our society, schools, co-workers, friends, and family about what we should or should not do with our lives and careers, and what is possible or not possible for us. We sometimes refer to these as "the shoulds." These external messages also shape our internal dialogue. That is, we talk to ourselves constantly about what we should or should not do or what we can or cannot do — this internal voice is called our "inner critic." These messages and judgments are not truth; they are merely perceptions. Although, most often, the intention is to keep us safe, these messages and judgments can limit the scope of what we think is possible for ourselves and what career options we choose to explore. They tend to create "noise" that prevents us from discovering what we really want for ourselves.

For the next few weeks, pay attention to the messages you are getting from the world around you and what you are saying to yourself. Write down what you notice below:

EXTERNAL JUDGMENTS

What my family, friends, school, work colleagues, and others think I should and should not do, and what is possible and not possible for me.

Examples:
"My mother said I'd make a great consultant."
"My friends think HR is too 'soft' a profession."
"Social media companies are really hot these days...."
"The right thing to do is to help the underprivileged."
"I spent all this money on law school; I should be a lawyer."

....
....
....
....

Which of these judgments tends to influence you the most?

....
....
....
....

If you pushed these judgments to the side, what would you consider doing?

....
....
....
....

Values

VALUES CLARIFICATION

Living our values in our work life is the key to fulfillment in our careers. So often, people have a work persona and a personal persona (that is, who they are at work and at home differ). The goal is to have these identities be the same by having them both reflect our values. It's what makes work not feel like work.

Values clarification is a process used to identify what is important to an individual, department, company, or for that matter, a country. When an individual is said to be true to his or her self, that self can be defined by a clear list of values. Not surprisingly, individuals' career satisfaction and fulfillment are much higher when they can express and realize many, if not all, of their personal values in their careers.

It is important to understand that values are not morals or ethics. Webster's Dictionary refers to a moral as "relating to principles of right and wrong behavior." Values, on the other hand, are "intrinsically valuable or desirable...that which belongs to the essential nature or constitution of a thing" (person, department, company). While people can decide about their morals, they already *are* their values. Values can also change over time. For many people, the value of security is not important in their early twenties, but is very important once they have a family.

How we express our values may also change over time. The value of adventure might be expressed by rock climbing and bungee jumping when one is younger, but at a later stage in life this same value of adventure may be expressed through world travel.

Being true to your values helps you escape the weight of the "shoulds" or the external messages and judgments that we referred to earlier on page 22. Values clarification is not a process where you choose what values you would like to have or should have. It is an honest assessment that looks at who you are, right now in your life. When you honestly assess your values, your next step becomes much clearer.

The exercises on the following pages will help you define and clarify your values. We recommend that you do them early in your career transition or job search process. The information these exercises yield will not only help you make career decisions that will be most fulfilling (*see pages 24–29*), but can also help focus your search and information-gathering process.

Values

PEAK EXPERIENCE EXERCISE

A simple way to identify your values is to think of peak experiences in your life — moments when you were thriving, felt alive or on top of the world, and were completely yourself. A peak experience may be a moment in time, like crossing a finish line, or a period of time like your college years. It may be personal or professional in nature, and may have occurred at *any* time in your life, including your childhood or adolescent years. By reflecting on the aspects of those experiences that made you feel this way, you can identify your values. For example, if a peak experience of yours was climbing a mountain, this may reflect the values of perseverance or challenge. A time when you learned Spanish in Guatemala may reflect the values of diversity, communication, or adventure. A time when you were part of a college musical may suggest the values of teamwork, creativity, or performance. A more detailed example of a peak experience and the apparent values reflected in that experience is as follows:

> *Several years ago, I decided to train for a triathlon. I had never been very athletic or in especially good shape but I just decided to go for it. Maybe that was part of my interest — to do something I wasn't sure I could do. I started training with some other people at my gym twice a week, as well as doing my own training. I liked the camaraderie of meeting new people, as well as having time to myself just to run, bike, swim, and think. It was amazingly time-intensive and coincided with a big rush at work but I had no problem getting everything done. I just became a lot more efficient. I was in constant pain for several weeks but I kept on going. I think I liked having a big project to sink my teeth into. In the end, not only did I finish the triathlon, but I was in the upper half of the finishers, which was a huge accomplishment for me.*

Some values that appear to be present in this example are:

- Performance
- Perseverance
- Self-improvement
- Big challenges
- Like-minded peers
- Support from others
- Time for myself
- Productivity
- Focus and discipline

Use the next page to describe some of your peak experiences and begin to articulate your values.

Values

PEAK EXPERIENCE EXERCISE

Describe in the space below one or two of your peak experiences. Where were you? Who were you with? What were you doing? Describe any details you can remember (i.e., the weather, the music in the background, etc.) that made this time so special. If possible, focus on nonprofessional experiences to avoid inadvertently incorporating values you think you "should" have.

Values

VALUES LIST *Think about one of your peak experiences described on the prior page. What core aspects made this experience so special? What values are present?*

1.
2.
3.
4.
5.
6.
7.
8.
9.
10.

If you examine several peak experiences, you will find that with each additional peak experience, there will be some overlap in the underlying values that are present, and each additional experience may shed light on other values. The bottom line is that these were your peak experiences because these were times when you were completely living your values. That is, you were being completely who you are! It is only when we are able to express our values that we can be who we really are — and therefore thrive and succeed!

After identifying your underlying values from your peak experiences, you may check the values list on *page 160–161* of the Appendix to see if there are any you may have missed. If you have not completed the peak experience exercise, we recommend that you go back and do so before looking at the list in order to generate your core values, as opposed to just choosing from a list.

Values

VALUES RANKING

Once you have identified your values, prioritize your top ten values, starting with the most important. A good way to determine the values that are most important is to ask yourself, *"Which value(s) would I be most miserable without?"*

1.
2.
3.
4.
5.
6.
7.
8.
9.
10.

We will revisit this list in *Part 4* when we discuss *Evaluating Job Offers (see pages 146–148)*.

Values

DIRECTIONS Using your values list from the previous page, label each bar below with a value that is important to you. When you have completed labeling each bar, rate the extent to which your current or prior job allowed you to live or express each value on a scale from 0 to 10, with 0 meaning *"I was not at all living this value,"* and 10 meaning *"I was completely living this value."* For example, you may have a value of autonomy and previously worked in a role as an individual contributor, which gave you a fair amount of autonomy. However, your boss may have been somewhat of a micromanager, so you might rate this value at a 7 overall for your last job.

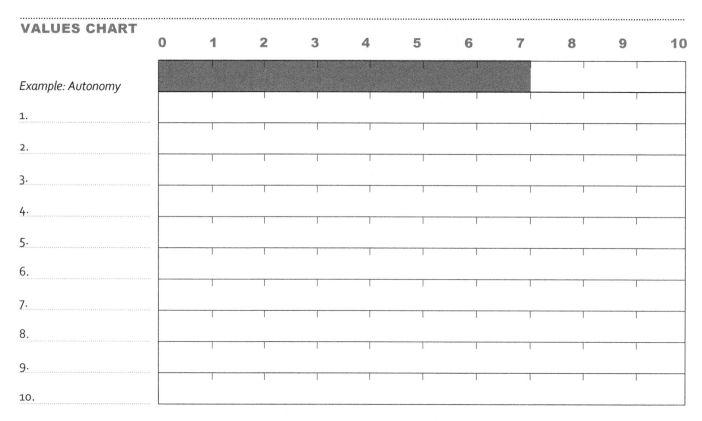

Your values rating of your most recent job should be indicative of your overall level of satisfaction or fulfillment in that job. For each value, ask yourself: What would a 10 look like (where a 10 represents your ideal amount of that value, not necessarily a lot of it)? What would the role need to be like to reach a 10?

The values listed in the above chart will also serve as an important screen — or decision-making criteria — when it comes time to evaluate actual job opportunities *(see page 146–148)*.

Values

TRANSLATING VALUES INTO QUESTIONS

In addition to helping you focus your job search, your list of values can inform the questions you should be asking in both informational interviews and job interviews. Essentially, taking into account your values will help ensure that you are collecting the *right* information throughout the course of your discussions. In a meaningful job search, the goal is not just to get a job — it's to get the right job for you — and the definition of what is right for you will depend on your own values.

Here are some examples of how you might pose questions related to specific personal values:

VALUE	POTENTIAL QUESTIONS
AUTONOMY	• To what extent would I be free to decide how to best approach specific projects? • Which decisions would I be primarily responsible for and which decisions would you expect me to ask you for guidance? • On a scale of 1–10, how much autonomy do you have at this company? In this department? In this job?
COLLABORATION	• On a scale of 1–10, how much does this work lend itself to collaboration? • How collaborative is this team? This department? This company? • What are some examples of projects where you collaborate across departments or functions?
INTELLECTUAL CHALLENGE	• What are the types of problems you are charged with solving? • What are some of the more complex problems or projects you've been working on? • What do you find intellectually challenging about your work? What do you find less challenging?
SUPPORT	• What type of training and development opportunities are available at this company? • What type of budget would I have to work with in this role? What other resources would be available to support me being successful? • What type of support do you provide to your team members?
RECOGNITION	• How are people typically recognized at your company for their work? • What's an example of a time you were recognized for something you did well at work? • How much do titles matter at this company? What are other ways that people's value is recognized?

Values

TRANSLATING VALUES INTO QUESTIONS For your top 10 values, draft some potential questions that you can use in informational interviews and job interviews, to provide additional insight into how much you'd be able to express those values in a given job, company, or career path.

VALUE	POTENTIAL QUESTIONS
1. _____	
2. _____	
3. _____	
4. _____	
5. _____	
6. _____	
7. _____	
8. _____	
9. _____	
10. _____	

Vision

"I shut my eyes in order to see" — Paul Gauguin

Creating a vision for our lives and careers involves tapping into our imaginations. If you have ever day-dreamed, you have likely envisioned something you want for yourself — for example, world travel, a family, work that has you viewed as an expert speaking at conferences, etc.

Vision takes time to create. The answers don't all come at once. A good metaphor is that of an artist's canvas — there is a splash of paint here, some more color or brushstrokes there, and over time, a clearer picture starts to form. In creating your vision, you may not see a whole lot at first. A practical way to approach vision is to simply ask yourself, *"What do I want in my life? In five years? In ten years?"*

When tapping into your vision, it is important to put aside both external judgments (e.g., *"You should leverage your banking experience to do corporate development"*) and your inner critic (e.g., *"You're too old to start a career in the entertainment industry"*), as both interfere with the creativity and imagination required. When it comes to exploring your vision, it is also important that you focus on the *what*, not the *how*. Questions about *how* you will achieve a specific career get in the way of fully defining *what* that career looks like. Until you define the *what*, you need to set aside the *how*.

Our visions are our own. By definition, they are vague. This can be frustrating for many people. It is not an analytical process in which if we just think harder, the answer will come to us.

The following exercises can help you gain greater clarity over time around your vision. Writing about what you see, and then talking about it with a coach or friend who can ask you clarifying questions, may also help you articulate more detail regarding the future you want to create.

Take time with these exercises. Developing and articulating a vision is an ongoing process. Build on your vision over time and enjoy the creative process!

VISION QUESTIONS

To create your vision, explore the answers to the following questions:

Where do you want to be in your work life in five years?

....

....

When you look at your life as a whole, what part do you want your career to play?

....

....

In what kind of environment do you want to work?

....

....

With whom do you want to work?

....

....

Vision

VISION QUESTIONS

What resources do you want to have?

What daily activities do you see yourself doing?

What experiences do you want to have?

In what other ways do you want to be growing and learning?

What is the kind of impact you want to have?

What do you see as the most productive or exciting aspect of your career?

What skills do you want to develop or refine?

What kind of recognition would you like to receive, and from whom?

At what pace do you want to work?

What type of schedule/work hours would you like to have?

Vision

Imagine yourself five years from today living a life that is satisfying and fulfilling. Imagine aspects of your life that relate to each of the three arenas outlined below. Complete the statement: *"Five years from now I want...."* Jot down your thoughts regarding what you want or see for yourself in the areas of your life that are indicated in each box.

PERSONAL LIFE	Home Surroundings Family Intimate Relationships Friendships
WORK LIFE	Workplace Activities Expertise Experiences Coworkers
CONTRIBUTION	Family Friends Work Community

Vision

OTHER EXERCISES

The process of developing a career vision requires an open mind and the engagement of your imagination. You are creating it ... just as you want it to be.

Here are some additional activities you can do to help develop and clarify your vision:

- Go for a walk and notice what catches your attention. What do these things tell you about what you are naturally drawn to and what you want in your future?
- Flip through magazines and pull out pictures and articles that represent what you want for your life and career five years from now. Maintain a file of these pictures and articles.
- Make a list of all the people you admire or envy. What about them or their lives would you like to incorporate in your life?

ATTRIBUTES OF YOUR VISION

Based on the preceding exercises that started on *page 31*, what are the primary attributes of your vision? If you imagine living overseas and managing a division of a growing company five years from now, you might list the following attributes: international career; manager of a large team; growing or innovative company. Extract specific attributes from your vision to help you evaluate how much job opportunities today will contribute to your picture of tomorrow.

1.
2.
3.
4.
5.
6.
7.
8.
9.
10.

We will revisit the attributes of your vision in *Part 4 — Evaluating Job Offers* (*see pages 146–148*).

Competencies

SKILLS, KNOWLEDGE, TRAITS

Your competencies are what you bring to an employer. Specifically, they are broad areas of expertise that encompass three major categories:

Skills: Specific things you can do and functions you can perform, such as "analyze risk factors" or "create marketing plans."

Knowledge: The functional and domain expertise you have developed, such as "small business market" or "valuation techniques."

Traits: The personal style and behaviors you display in your professional life, such as "calm under pressure" or "direct and assertive."

Documenting your skills, knowledge, and traits is a helpful step to determine which career(s) you may be best suited for, and will help ensure that you clearly communicate your ability to contribute to potential employers. To determine your competencies and prepare to communicate them to a potential employer, take the following steps.

DETERMINING YOUR COMPETENCIES

Step 1: Identify Your Accomplishments

Make a list of your accomplishments (both personal and professional). Give yourself some time to create this list. Don't discount personal accomplishments — these can be just as indicative of your competencies. The following questions may help you identify some of your professional accomplishments:

- *What problems did you identify and solve?*
- *What new program, product, or system did you introduce?*
- *How did you save the organization money or time? How much?*
- *How much did you contribute to revenues or profits?*
- *How did you effectively manage others?*
- *In what decision making or planning did you participate?*
- *What awards, bonuses, or promotions did you receive?*
- *What challenges(s) have you overcome?*

Step 2: Highlight Specific Accomplishments

Identify the accomplishments that you are:

- *Most proud of*
- *Most excited about*
- *Really enjoyed*

Step 3: Analyze Your Accomplishments

Look at each of your highlighted accomplishments and determine:

- *The skills you used; the actions you had to take to get these results*
- *The knowledge that you gained or applied*
- *The traits you demonstrated*

Step 4: Describe Your Competencies

- *What can you do that is unique and sets you apart?*
- *What is highly appealing to the marketplace and your potential employers?*
- *What combination of skills, knowledge, and traits is required to achieve the specific results that a particular employer is looking for?*

See pages 123–127 on how to communicate your competencies in an interview.

Competencies

COMPETENCY WORKSHEET

Step 1: Identify Your Accomplishments

Examples:

"Increased profitability of two dental hygiene product lines by more than 50% through product repositioning and enhanced marketing efforts."

"Trained for and completed New York Marathon."

"Promoted ahead of schedule to Senior Manager at my last company."

"Self-financed undergraduate degree while working part-time."

"Helped an underprivileged family keep their apartment in a pro bono case."

....

....

....

....

....

....

....

....

....

....

Step 2: Highlight Specific Accomplishments

In the list above, highlight four accomplishments that you:

- Are most proud of
- Are most excited about
- Really enjoyed

Competencies

COMPETENCY WORKSHEET

Step 3: Analyze Your Accomplishments
Describe the skills, knowledge, and traits you used in each of your highlighted accomplishments.

Accomplishment 1
Example: Increased profitability of two dental hygiene product lines by more than 50% through product repositioning and enhanced marketing efforts

....

....

....

....

Skills
Example: Analytical skills

....

....

....

....

Knowledge
Example: Knowledge of target markets, market research techniques, and dental hygiene industry

....

....

....

....

Traits
Example: Self-starter, creative

....

....

....

....

Competencies

COMPETENCY WORKSHEET

Accomplishment 2

....
....
....
....
....

Skills

....
....
....
....
....

Knowledge

....
....
....
....
....

Traits

....
....
....
....
....

Competencies

COMPETENCY WORKSHEET

Accomplishment 3

....

....

....

....

....

Skills

....

....

....

....

....

Knowledge

....

....

....

....

....

Traits

....

....

....

....

....

Competencies

COMPETENCY WORKSHEET

Accomplishment 4

....

....

....

....

....

Skills

....

....

....

....

....

Knowledge

....

....

....

....

....

Traits

....

....

....

....

....

Assessment Tools

There are a variety of career and personality assessments available to assist you in your career transition and career development. Assessments should *never* be relied upon to supply an answer for what you should be doing next. Rather, their purpose is to provide a variety of data points to prompt further reflection and exploration. Assessment results may do nothing more than affirm what you like or don't like, which can still be helpful information. They may also highlight new areas to consider or provide other information for you to react to. Some assessments, such as the Myers Briggs Type Indicator® and the Strong Interest Inventory®, described below, need to be administered and interpreted by a qualified professional. Other assessments, such as Career Leader®, can be taken online, allowing you to see your results immediately. Nonetheless, you may still want to review the results with a career coach.

More detailed descriptions of these assessments follow.

ASSESSMENT DESCRIPTIONS

Myers Briggs Type Indicator® (MBTI), Step II

This personality assessment measures your innate personality preferences in terms of how you derive energy, take in information, make decisions, and operate in the world. Your personality type has unique implications for how you communicate, deal with change, lead or manage others, solve problems, and how you interact with others who are of different personality types. Understanding your own personality type, as well as the personality types of others, can help you to be more productive as a leader, manager, and co-worker. Moreover, your personality type will likely also have implications on your career choice and how you manage the career transition process.

Strong Interest Inventory®

Based upon your indicated interests, this assessment helps identify general occupational themes, as well as points to specific occupations of people who share similar interests and are highly satisfied in their careers. Personal styles with respect to work, learning, leadership, and risk taking are also examined.

Career Leader®

This career tool, developed by Harvard Business School career psychologists, is widely used to provide an expert assessment of unique patterns of business-relevant interests, values, and abilities. Career Leader® includes three tests and recommends specific *business-oriented* career paths that are likely to be your best career path matches. In addition, the assessment provides you with in-depth views into more than 20 business career paths, including information about the interests, rewards, and abilities associated with each one. Many of the career paths profiled also include an in-depth interview with an industry insider.

Mini-360 Assessment

If you are unsure of what's next for you, another type of assessment or source of data about what you would be good at or enjoy is to conduct a "mini-360" of friends and colleagues who know you well. This can be done with as few as 3–5 people or as many as 10–20 people or more. The more responses to the survey you receive, the more easily you will be able to identify trends in the responses. You will also want to take into account that not everyone will get back to you in a timely manner (or potentially at all), so you'll want to err on the side of asking more people to participate than responses you hope to receive. Asking 10–15 people to participate will probably get you a good amount of responses. This can be done with the questions embedded in an email or in an online survey at a site like SurveyMonkey.

Keep in mind that the information you receive is helpful in that it shows other people's perspectives of you, but be careful not to succumb to "the shoulds," as referenced on *page 22* in the *Outside Influences* exercise. As with other assessments, do not rely on the mini-360 to provide you with an answer, but rather, look at the results as interesting data to react to and reflect upon.

You might send an introductory email, that says something like:

> To: Friends and Colleagues
> From: Arden White
> Subject: My Next Career Move
>
> Friends and Colleagues,
>
> I am currently exploring my next career move and would greatly value your input on a small number of questions – your answers to which will be very helpful for me to reflect on, as I consider what's next for me professionally. It should only take you 5-10 minutes, maximum. I'd really appreciate your feedback since you know me quite well. If you could complete the questions (or survey) below by [insert date one week from when you send your email], that would be great.
>
> Thanks in advance for your participation!
>
> All the best,
>
> Arden

You may need to send a reminder email a day or two before your desired response date.

Mini-360 Assessment

POTENTIAL QUESTIONS TO INCLUDE

Below are a number of questions from which you can choose. In keeping to the 5–10 minute response guideline, you will want to keep the survey brief. You may also answer the questions below as a self-assessment and compare your responses to the answers you receive.

1) What three adjectives would you use to describe me?

2) What do you see as my greatest strengths or talents?

3) What are the skills that, if acquired or developed further, would most benefit me in my career?

4) In what types of situations am I at my best?

5) What have you seen me get most excited about?

6) In what type of jobs/positions/careers do you think I would thrive the most (and why)?

7) What types of jobs/positions/industries do you think I would not enjoy (and why)?

Mini-360 Assessment

REVIEWING RESPONSES

Once you've collected all of the responses, answer the following questions:

What are the common themes?

Which of these themes resonate with me or feel true?

Which themes don't resonate with me or feel as true?

Where do I sense that the answers reflect some of "the shoulds" that most often arise for me?

What avenues do the responses suggest that I explore?

What follow-up questions do I have based on the responses and whom do I want to reach out to in order to probe deeper into the responses?

Describing Your Brand

Before conducting a job search, take a step back and look at the bigger picture of where you currently are in your career and where you want to go. As with products, services, and organizations, being clear about your brand — who you are, what others see in you, and what you want to be known for in the future — can help guide your planning and decision making.

Like a physical product, we each have our own personal brand. Just as a Jeep Cherokee is known for something different than a Porsche (a rugged family car versus a sleek sports car), individuals have brands that differ from each other. One individual may be known as a workhorse who rolls up his or her sleeves to get a job done, and another may be known as a highly creative visionary. Likewise, Donald Trump and Mark Zuckerberg are both entrepreneurs but have very different brands.

Assess how you are seen by others professionally now and how you would like to be seen in the future, so that you can intentionally guide the development of your brand and your resulting reputation.

When answering the first question below, your current identity or reputation, imagine that your name comes up in conversation among your colleagues and you are absent. What are they saying about you? Great client skills? Good listener? Forward-looking?

In answering the second question below, your desired future identity or reputation, don't get stuck initially in *what* it is that you want to be doing — this question is more about the *manner* in which you will do whatever it is that you do in the future. For example, you may aspire to be a CFO. Do you want to be known as the CFO who comes up with highly innovative financing solutions? The CFO who is an expert in taking companies public? The CFO who focuses on the training and development of his or her team? Likewise, you don't have to know *what* you want to do to know what you want to be known for. You can also review various aspects of your vision from *pages 31–34* to see how that adds to or informs your brand.

CURRENT IDENTITY / REPUTATION	*What are you known for now?*
DESIRED FUTURE IDENTITY / REPUTATION	*What do you want to be known for in five years that you are not known for now?*

Describing Your Brand

BRAND REPOSITIONING EXAMPLE

Your brand evolution will have an impact on many things — from the activities you undertake while still in school or outside of work to the positions or career that you seek. Let's look at an example.

Current Identity or Reputation	Colleagues currently think of me as being a highly analytical engineer who writes excellent software.
Desired Future Identity or Reputation	I want to be known as someone who has a social conscience and is committed to improving the quality of life for others.

Clarifying Your Future Brand

Our desired future identity or reputation is, in essence, part of our vision. The example above is a good start. To get even clearer about our future identity or reputation, here are some open-ended, follow-up questions to ask in this example.

As a part of this future identity:

- How are you improving the quality of life for others? (i.e., through technology, social entrepreneurship, humanitarian efforts?)
- Who are the people for whom you want to improve the quality of life? (i.e., people in your local community, under-privileged youth, a national population, or people in certain developing countries?)
- Who knows you as someone with a social conscience? (i.e., your immediate colleagues, your broader local community, the national population, or even an international audience?)
- What cause do you see furthering that will improve the quality of other people's lives? (i.e., education, literacy, malnutrition, anti-violence programs, or something else?)

Repositioning Your Brand

After prompting by these probing questions, let's suppose this individual wants to improve the quality of life for at-risk youth through creating local after-school programs that educate teens in technology. At first, he or she is known in the local community as a social entrepreneur. Eventually, the program will expand nationally, gaining more funding for scholarships.

Now, what are the implications of this desired brand shift for an individual while in the job search? There are many — let's start with the following questions:

- What are you doing/not doing that keeps you stuck in your current identity or reputation?
- What can you start/stop doing so you will be seen in the way you desire?
- How do you talk about yourself to others so that they will see you in the desired way?
- What classes might you take to help make this shift happen?
- What projects can you undertake?
- What organizations can you join?
- What other extracurricular activities (e.g., volunteering) can help you make this shift?
- What positions, organizations, or careers are consistent with your desired identity or reputation?
- Which people have a brand similar to the one you desire, that you can talk to in order to learn how they got there?

Describing Your Brand

We encourage you to do the previous exercise with a coach, friend, or colleague. Having someone else to ask you clarifying questions can help you to better articulate what you are striving for. This greater level of clarity will help you move into action.

Continuing with the prior example, we can incorporate our values, talents, and interests into our desired brand evolution to create a brand statement, as illustrated below.

VALUES	*What are the core values you live by?* My core values include creating opportunities for others, risk taking, autonomy, and contributing to society.
TALENTS & INTERESTS	*What are your greatest talents or abilities? What interests you the most?* My talents include writing software, strong analytical skills, and good organizational skills. My interests are primarily in the realm of social entrepreneurship and education.
BRAND STATEMENT	*Summarize your answers to all of the questions above in a brief brand statement.* In my work, I value taking risks to create opportunities for others and working autonomously to make a social contribution. I bring my talents of strong technological knowledge and organizational skills to helping others. In my next role, I would like to be thought of as someone with a social conscience who is committed to improving the quality of life for others. Five years from now, I would like to be a social entrepreneur, dedicated to helping at-risk teens through after-school programs that educate them in technology.

Describing Your Brand

After completing the questions on your brand evolution on *page 45*, and exploring specific aspects of that evolution, fill in the boxes below to come up with your personal brand statement. You may reference your values noted on *page 26* and your competencies on *pages 35–40* for this exercise.

VALUES	*What are the core values you live by?*
TALENTS & INTERESTS	*What are your greatest talents or abilities? What interests you the most?*
BRAND STATEMENT	*Summarize your answers to all of the questions above in a brief brand statement.*

PART

3

Career Exploration

The Exploration Process

The next step in your career is an important one. The exploration process to determine what this step is can be overwhelming. The future represents a great frontier with endless possibilities — which can be both exciting and daunting. Where on earth do you start?

When it comes to what you want to do next, you will likely fall into one of three main categories: (1) you have no idea what you want to do, (2) you are considering a few potential paths, or (3) you have a fairly clear idea of what you want.

You have no idea what you want to do

If you fall into the first category — never fear, you are not alone! Many people get stuck in this process because they feel that to start a job search, they need to know precisely what they want. While this information is certainly helpful, it is not at all necessary as a starting point. The irony is that while many people hold themselves back from moving into action because they don't have "the answer" — they will, in fact, only find the answer by moving into action!

The exploration process is highly iterative and involves much experimentation (*see page 52*), as well as a certain amount of trial and error as you collect information from various sources. The collection of such information can take various forms, such as talking to colleagues, former classmates, and friends of friends; going to a conference; joining an industry association; taking a new class; reading a book; or doing a volunteer project, to name a few. *Networking* and *Informational Interviews*, which are addressed on *pages 56–67* and *77–82*, respectively, are key parts of the exploration process.

Negative information, defined as information that diminishes one's interest in a given path, is just as useful as positive information, or information that reinforces one's interest in a particular path. As we collect information on various jobs or careers, we can ask ourselves the following questions:

- Can I see myself doing this type of work?
- Can I see myself working in this type of environment?
- Can I see myself working with colleagues like these?
- Can I see myself living this kind of lifestyle?

There are countless other such questions that we can ask. We then sort through the information, perhaps with the assistance of a good coach, friend, or colleague. Note that none of these people should ever tell you what you *should* do. Instead, they can act as a sounding board in addition to asking you good probing questions and reflecting back to you what they are noticing (e.g., "*I can see you are really excited by this field. What excites you the most?*").

A good analogy for this part of the process is that of trying on new clothes. Do these new clothes reflect who you are? Feel right? Look good? Represent something you will want to wear one year from now? Three years from now? Perhaps the pants fit you well, but you don't like the top? That is, perhaps one part of the profession appeals to you, but not other parts. Through this exploration, you will eventually find a few potential paths worth dedicating more time to.

We recommend exploring only one to two potential career paths at a time, depending on how much time you have to dedicate to the career transition and job search process.

The Exploration Process

Through this process of collecting information and sorting through it, we can start to close some doors and narrow our focus. This may be difficult or scary for some people (we find this is often the case with former consultants who entered consulting for the very reason that it left so many options open to them). If you find after much exploration that you are having difficulty narrowing your options and are experiencing great indecision — and thus a prolonged and unproductive search — we encourage you to seek help from a coach or your Career Center if you are in a part-time or executive degree program.

You are considering a few potential paths

Much of the above-described exploration also applies to those who have a few potential paths in mind. For these individuals, the exploration process is somewhat more focused, as each potential path provides a more tangible starting point. The alternative paths may be tangentially related (such as private equity and other forms of investing like venture capital) or they may be quite different (such as consumer marketing and investor relations).

In either case, your goal may be to ultimately focus on just one path, eliminating one or more existing potential paths, or your goal may be to find an attractive opportunity in any one of the few equally desirable paths that you have identified.

You have a fairly clear idea of what you want

If you fall into this category, your exploration process will revolve around answering the following questions:

- Am I *sure* that this is the path that I want? How do I know?
- Do *I* want this or does someone else want this for me? (*See page 22 on Outside Influences.*)
- What related (or different) fields have I not considered that warrant examining?
- What companies or positions in this field offer the best opportunities and fit with my core strengths and values?

The first two questions are related to obtaining affirmation that your chosen path is indeed the one you want, independent of what others think. Further, before committing to a path, are there aspects of the career that you were not aware of previously? Have you done ample due diligence?

Focus can give you a great head start in the search process. Nonetheless, it may be valuable to take time to explore what opportunities might also be equally or even more satisfying and fulfilling to you that you either didn't know about or haven't considered previously.

Once you have the affirmation you need about your desired path, the exploration process will revolve around finding the best possible role and organization where you can build your career.

Experimentation

Experimentation is a key part of the exploration process and is how we check out how well our ideas correspond to reality. Experimenting is test driving a car before you buy it. It's inhabiting a role temporarily to see what it's like. It's testing a hypothesis to see if it flies. Experimentation is about doing — not thinking. Experimentation opens us up to new ideas and possibilities while providing valuable information with which to make career and life choices. It allows us to expand or narrow our focus, as needed. Implicit in experimentation is the notion that any information is good information.

Examples of Experiments
- Reading a book or article on a new subject
- Talking through an idea with a friend
- Conducting an informational interview
- Having a job interview
- Shadowing someone at their job for a day
- Taking a class
- Attending a conference
- Going to a professional event
- Writing an article
- Hanging out with new people
- Developing a business plan
- Advising a start-up
- Volunteering
- Being a consultant
- Serving on a board or committee
- Traveling to a new city

CREATE EXPERIMENTS

Exercise: *Consider one of the career interests you have. Write down 10 potential experiments you could undertake to gain more information about this area of interest.*

1.
2.
3.
4.
5.
6.
7.
8.
9.
10.

Positioning Statement

Regardless of your focus (or lack of it, as the case may be), you need to be able to talk about yourself in an effective way that inspires others' confidence in you and invites them to assist you in some way, no matter how small.

Your positioning statement is a key element of your communications strategy. It is a concise statement that provides a snapshot of you and gives your audience an immediate sense of who you are, what you are known for, what you are considering doing next, and how they can help you.

It is a great answer to questions like:

- *Tell me about yourself.*
- *What do you do?*
- *What are you looking for?*
- *What have you been up to since I last saw you?*

Remember to be succinct — but make your positioning statement interesting enough to inspire questions from the other person and prompt a dialogue to allow you the opportunity to elaborate.

The statement includes:

- Your professional identity
- The most relevant, compelling, and unique elements of your experience and areas of strength; the problems you are good at solving; the work you love to do that you want to do more of; or what you are known for
- The types and brand names of the organizations where you have worked or would like to work
- The opportunities or information you are looking for to further your experience and take the next step in your career.

Positioning statements can be written, such as would be used in a cover letter or email introduction, or they can be spoken. For the job search, it is vital that you develop a fluid, concise, understandable, and interesting spoken positioning statement that you can use in everyday conversations with people. Spoken positioning statements are slightly different from written positioning statements in that they use somewhat less formal language.

Positioning statements are not just for official job-search interactions. Imagine meeting someone at a dinner party, a basketball game, the gym, or on a plane who says, *"Nice to meet you. So, what do you do?"* What would you say about yourself? You might run into an old friend or acquaintance who asks, *"So, what have you been up to?"* Your positioning statement, tailored to fit the audience and the question that is asked, is the ideal answer.

Positioning Statement

Below are examples of both written and spoken positioning statements.

WRITTEN EXAMPLES

"Most recently, I worked for Coca Cola where I conducted focus group research that contributed to the successful launch of several new products. I am now looking to apply my education and experience to a research position with a consumer-oriented financial services company such as American Express, Visa, or Charles Schwab."

"I am a management consultant with experience in strategy and planning for biotech companies. I have been particularly effective working with growing companies to develop strategies to increase revenues and profitability. I am currently pursuing an Executive MBA and would like to apply my skills to a strategy role at a leading biotech or pharmaceutical company."

"I am currently an investment banker with four years of mergers and acquisitions experience at Morgan Stanley. I have worked on multiple $100 million+ transactions for companies and have provided general financial advisory services. I am looking to transfer my finance and transaction skills to a business development role in a small to mid-size technology company in the Boston area."

SPOKEN EXAMPLES

"I am currently an English teacher and am pursuing a part-time MBA. I am interested in opportunities in education and now want to apply what I know about education and business management to a role at a university."

"I previously worked at Bain, where I focused on consumer products clients. I plan on relocating to Seattle to be closer to my family, so I am currently looking for strategy roles at consumer products companies in the area, such as Starbucks, Nordstrom, or Amazon."

"I am a commercial loan officer at Bank of America. Getting involved in various women's causes this year has really inspired me to leverage my banking experience to help women in developing countries, so I am looking for opportunities at microfinance organizations, and would love to talk with people who work in this field."

EXPLORATORY EXAMPLES

Even if you are unclear of your direction, you *can and should* still have a positioning statement. As mentioned earlier, a key part of a positioning statement is to inspire others' confidence in you and to enlist their help and support. Even if you are feeling lost, you need to have an exploratory positioning statement to show that you are organized and thoughtful about the process, and inspire confidence. Moreover, not saying anything about yourself is a missed opportunity! A good exploratory positioning statement may elicit helpful information and contacts required to help you obtain clarity and move forward in your search. Below are some examples of such positioning statements:

"I previously worked in investment banking at Goldman Sachs. What I liked most was the client service aspect of my job. As a result, I am exploring other fields that are client service focused, such as investor relations, consulting, and investment management for high net worth individuals."

"While I have a background in high-tech marketing, pursuing a part-time MBA has introduced me to many new areas. I'm currently exploring a few potential paths, including educational technology and brand management."

"I am currently in transition and am exploring various options. Right now, I am researching careers in the entertainment and social media industries and would love to talk to people who work in either of these sectors."

"I have a background in finance and worked at Wells Fargo for 10 years before taking time off to have a family. I am exploring temporary or part-time options, as I am now looking to go back to work. I'd love to talk to other people who have gone back to work after taking time off."

Positioning Statement

What's your positioning statement? You may have more than one that you use depending on your audience or the path(s) that you are pursuing. Use the following space to draft your positioning statement(s).

Draft 1

Draft 2

Draft 3

Finished Positioning Statement(s)

Networking

BUILDING RELATIONSHIPS

Networking, the process of building relationships, is crucial throughout your career, particularly when you are looking for a job. It is through networking that you are likely to find your next job. According to the US Bureau of Labor Statistics, 70% of all jobs are found through networking — other sources estimate this figure at 80–85%. Since many jobs are not formally advertised or posted, networking allows you to tap into this hidden job market, giving you access to needed resources, information, and opportunities — so you want to do it well!

Many people in your career have likely emphasized the importance of networking. However, many professionals end up with an overly limited definition of networking, associating it exclusively with large job fairs or recruiting events, where there are scores of job seekers and only a few company representatives. This definition of networking can leave you feeling discouraged, with a negative view of this important activity.

In reality, networking goes well beyond these job fairs or recruiting events to include any social interaction with another person. This more expansive definition creates room for multiple perspectives on networking. Your individual perspective on this topic is important in that it will directly influence your networking behaviors — which will, in turn, affect your outcomes.

For example, if you start with the perspective that networking is manipulative (which, when done poorly, it certainly can be), you will likely be reluctant to engage in networking activities. In contrast, holding a perspective that networking is fun will lead you to engage in activities where you may meet others and discuss similar interests.

There are an infinite number of perspectives on networking. In addition to the two mentioned above (networking is manipulative and networking is fun), here are some others that include both positive and negative perspectives:

- *Only extroverts are good at networking*
- *Networking can lead to the unexpected!*
- *Networking is like a treasure hunt*
- *Networking is not worth the hassle*

Come up with some additional perspectives on networking. For example, what do you think Donald Trump's perspective is on networking? Bill Clinton's? Oprah Winfrey's? See how many perspectives you can come up with. Discuss with a group of friends or colleagues various perspectives, what each has to offer you and how adopting each perspective would affect your networking behavior.

1.
2.
3.
4.
5.
6.
7.

Networking

After you have identified various perspectives on networking, choose one positive perspective that you will adopt for the next week. From this perspective, what actions will you take with respect to networking?

....

....

....

....

....

....

EFFECTIVE NETWORKING

Networking is most effective when it is done authentically. Think about a time when someone tried to network with you and he or she did it really well. What exactly did the person do (or not do, as the case may be)?

....

....

....

....

....

....

Networking

STRONG TIES VERSUS WEAK TIES

Before we dive into creating a networking plan, let's define some key terms. In *The Strength of Weak Ties*, published in the *American Journal of Sociology* in 1973, Professor Mark Granovetter — an expert in economic sociology at Stanford — established the concept of strong and weak ties. Strong ties represent relationships with individuals where there is an ongoing exchange of some kind. These are likely to be your family, close friends and colleagues, etc. Weak ties represent relationships with individuals where there is mutual recognition (you know them and they know you) but any kind of regular exchange is absent — for example, a former boss with whom you have been out of touch. Weak ties may also include people that you know tangentially, such as a friend of a friend.

In other research by Granovetter entitled *Getting a Job: A Study of Contacts and Careers*, he established that individuals who rely on their weak-tie networks to find a job (as opposed to their strong-tie networks) find higher paying jobs, obtain higher occupational status, and have greater job satisfaction and longer job tenure.

Why are our weak ties so valuable in a job search? First, our strong-tie networks have much of the same information we have. By tapping into new information and resources in our weak-tie networks, we find new opportunities. The value of one's weak-tie network is in the access to information and resources that these people can potentially provide either themselves, or through access to their own networks, to which we otherwise wouldn't have access.

In addition to Granovetter's above explanation of the value of weak ties, another reason our weak ties can be so helpful is that they don't necessarily see us in the "old" way that our strong ties see us. Thus, when it comes to changing careers, or evolving our personal brands, our weak ties are more open to seeing us how we currently choose to present ourselves — which is hopefully consistent with our desired future identity or reputation. For example, look back at the case illustrated on *page 46*. This former engineer's strong ties may see him strictly as someone who is analytical and writes flawless code, but not as the social entrepreneur that he wants to become.
In contrast, his weak ties have little or no attachment to a prior identity or personal brand and, thus, are more open to seeing him in the way he would like to be seen.

CREATING A NETWORKING PLAN

In the following pages, we map out four key steps in creating a coherent networking plan:

Step 1: Map Your Current Network

Step 2: Assess and Evaluate Your Network

Step 3: Expand and Maintain Your Network

Step 4: Access Your Network

Networking

STEP 1

Map Your Current Network

Use the Networking "Radar Screen" below to map or plot your existing network. Put the names of individuals in your network into the appropriate ring. Do this for as many people as come to mind.

Networking

STEP 2

Assess and Evaluate Your Network

Once you have mapped your current network, think about what it should look like, given your current short- and long-term career goals. How different is this network from the one you've visually mapped out?

Some key questions to ask in assessing and evaluating your network are:

- *Is my current network consistent with my career goals?*
- *Where am I "underinvested" in key relationships?*
- *Who is not currently on my radar screen that I would like to reconnect with or meet?*
- *Where am I "overinvested" and need to spend less time?*
- *Who do I want to get to know better?*
- *What are the 10 most crucial relationships I want to establish or cultivate in the next 12 months?*

The following pages show a sample assessment of an individual's network, as well as a blank template for you to complete based on your own network.

Networking

Sample Networking Assessment

POSITIONING STATEMENT	My specific career focus, or what I want to investigate
	I have a real estate background and have worked as a project manager in construction and development of residential and commercial properties. I am now looking to enter the investment side of real estate to work for a real estate investment fund.

CAREER GOALS	Short-term career goal (0–3 years)
	To obtain an associate-level position with a real estate investment fund that invests in properties across the country.
	Long-term career goal (5–10 years)
	To use my industry and acquired investment knowledge to source deals as a partner at a small to mid-sized real estate investment fund that invests globally, or to start my own fund with a few like-minded colleagues.

EXISTING NETWORK ASSESSMENT	Strong ties	Weak ties	Weaker ties
	• Officemate from last job • Charles Holloway (friend who knows everyone) • Janet K. • Rajiv S. (works for a big real estate fund) • Sister in Atlanta	• Prof. Townshend (real estate professor) • Friend from high school, now in real estate • Former colleagues from other jobs • Neighbor who left a real estate investment job	• J. Abbott (met on flight to London) • Prof. Barnes (investment guru, never met) • Author of Never Eat Alone • Mom's friend whose daughter works at a REIT

What's working in my network?

Know people from all walks of life

Have contacts in various cities

Know people who know people who work in the field

Have some contact with influential people

What's not working in my network? Where am I overinvested? Where am I underinvested?

Hanging out too much with people from construction

Need more investment contacts

Don't know many people in the investment management world

Given my career goals, what kinds of people should be in my network?

More people who currently work, or used to work, for my targeted firms or in areas I want to explore

Influential people who know the real estate investing industry

People who have done real estate investing in the U.S. or overseas (or both!)

People who are well-connected and better at networking than I am

Networking

Networking Assessment Template

POSITIONING STATEMENT	My specific career focus, or what I want to investigate			
CAREER GOALS	Short-term career goal (0–3 years) Long-term career goal (5–10 years)			
EXISTING NETWORK ASSESSMENT	Strong ties	Weak ties	Weaker ties
	What's working in my network? What's not working in my network? Where am I overinvested? Where am I underinvested? Given my career goals, what kinds of people should be in my network?		

Networking

STEP 3 — **Expand and Maintain Your Network**

A key step in creating a networking plan is to strategically identify ways to expand your network — that is, bridge the gap between the current state of your network and what you want it to look like. This involves making clear plans and commitments, using your positioning statement (*see pages 53–55*), focusing on weak ties, and establishing accountability structures. A sample action plan is provided below, along with a blank template and a matrix on the following pages, that allows you to think through ways to expand and maintain your network.

Sample Networking Action Plan

EXISTING NETWORK ASSESSMENT	**People to connect with:** ● Maria who works for a REIT ● My friend Bob who recently left real estate ● People who have made the transition from construction and development to real estate investing ● Ronald, who works at Hines	**Organizations to join:** ● National Association of Real Estate Investment Managers ● Local Real Estate Investment Association (REIA) ● National Association of Real Estate Investment Trusts ● Women in Real Estate LinkedIn group	**Ways to improve networking skills:** ● Go to Chamber of Commerce networking events ● Ask friends for referrals ● Practice my positioning statement ● Introduce myself to others ● Be curious — ask others questions about themselves
SPECIFIC PLANS & COMMITMENTS	**Networking structures (daily, weekly, or monthly):** Plan one lunch per week with people I don't know very well Spend two hours per week making calls and/or doing research Email or call one old friend per week that I haven't spoken to in a long time Attend one real estate industry event per month Spend 10 minutes/day connecting with people in real estate on LinkedIn		
FOCUS ON WEAK TIES	**The five weak ties I will reach out to in the next month are:** 1. Professor Townshend (my old real estate professor) 2. My cousin's friend who lives in Dallas 3. Samantha Briggs (president of the local REIA chapter) 4. Ronald Kim who works at Hines 5. Keith Ferrazzi, the author of Never Eat Alone **The one weak tie that I will call or email TODAY that I have not spoken to in over one year is:** 1. Tara Harrison — my mentor from my first job after college		
PERSONAL ACCOUNTABILITY	**To keep myself accountable, I will:** Review and revise this strategy once a month Get together with my friend Steve, who is also looking for a new job, every two weeks to go over our networking progress		

©2014 Next Step Partners | www.NextStepPartners.com

Networking

Networking Action Plan Template

EXISTING NETWORK ASSESSMENT	People to connect with:	Organizations to join:	Ways to improve networking skills:
SPECIFIC PLANS & COMMITMENTS	Networking structures (daily, weekly, or monthly):		
FOCUS ON WEAK TIES	The five weak ties I will reach out to in the next month are: 1. 2. 3. 4. 5. The one weak tie that I will call or email TODAY that I have not spoken to in over one year is: 1.		
PERSONAL ACCOUNTABILITY	To keep myself accountable, I will:		

Networking

It is not enough to build your network — you need to maintain it. Once you have assessed your current network and begun the planning process, use the matrix below to plot your strong and weak ties according to the frequency and depth of interaction you would like to achieve or maintain with each individual.

Networking Matrix

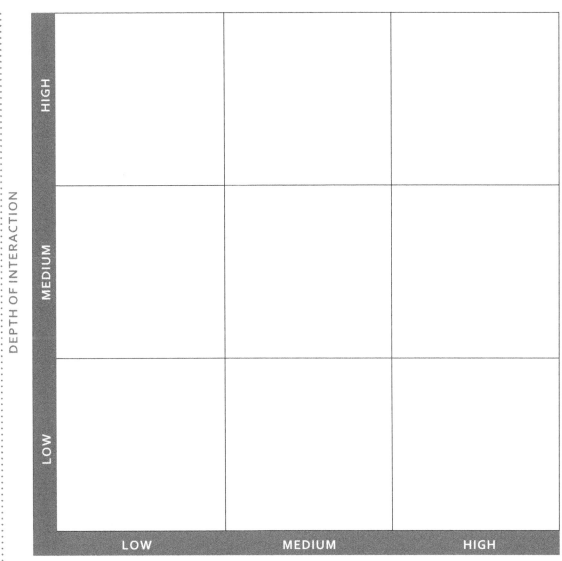

Contacts in the box "Low Frequency/Low Depth" might be on your holiday card list, whereas contacts in the box "Low Frequency/High Depth" might be people you vacation with. Likewise, someone who you would like to meet for lunch a few times a year might appear in the "Medium Frequency/Medium Depth" box. Once you have plotted your contacts in each quadrant, you can determine the type of contact or activity that is most appropriate.

Networking

STAYING NETWORKED

What many people don't recognize, until they are faced with a job search, is that it pays to *stay networked* — particularly in good times, when you don't feel the need as much to keep in touch. Maintaining your network on a regular basis will put you steps ahead of everyone else who has not remained connected when it comes time for a job search or getting the information or resources you need.

While most people are happy to help you by either taking time to meet with you or spending a few minutes to chat on the phone, their time is limited — and no one likes a fair-weather friend, acquaintance, or colleague. It can be uncomfortable for both parties to become reconnected only when one person needs something from the other.

Aside from the obvious efforts to join industry associations and other organizations, or contact alumni from your undergraduate or graduate universities, there are some simple, yet *highly effective,* ways to stay connected and build stronger professional relationships.

SIMPLE WAYS TO STAY CONNECTED

Let others know what you're up to

This can be done easily by email or in a holiday card. For example: *"I recently relocated to Chicago and will be working at American Express"* or *"My volunteer work helping low-income students to gain admission into college has reinforced my interest in educational causes. I will be relocating to New York after the winter holidays and am looking for an executive director position at an educational non-profit...."* By letting others know what you are up to, you are not only inviting them to assist you, but you are also letting them know that you'd like to keep in touch with them. Most will be flattered that you kept them up to date and won't be as surprised to hear from you if you do call them in the future for a favor.

Go to lunch

It's easy to get consumed with your work and just inhale a sandwich at your desk. However, by making a point to go to lunch at least once or twice a week (if not more frequently) with a colleague, friend, or acquaintance in the working community, you not only stay in touch, but you also find out what's been happening with other people and organizations.

Call friends and colleagues when you are traveling

Not only does this beat eating a cold sandwich in your hotel room, it is also a great way to stay in touch and find out what's going on with others. Be sure to reciprocate the invitation when they are in your city on business or holiday.

Take leadership positions

Whether it is at your place of worship, in an industry association, or in planning a conference, assuming a leadership position gives you the ability to (1) meet diverse groups of professionals, (2) be seen and known by others, and (3) call members of these groups and ask them for information, help, etc.

Use social media

Connecting with friends, acquaintances, classmates, and colleagues on Facebook, Twitter, or LinkedIn is also a good way to stay in touch. Liking or commenting on a post, saying "Happy Birthday," or congratulating someone on a new job or work anniversary is another small, but effective, way to stay connected.

Networking

SIMPLE WAYS TO STAY CONNECTED

Give others something they need

This can be done unsolicited or when someone asks for your help. Put people in contact with a potential employer, client or partners, or give them information that could be useful to them, and they will remember your generosity and return the favor. For example, by sending people information on an upcoming conference in their field that they may not already be aware of, with a note attached saying, *"I thought you might be interested in this..."*, you remind them of your presence and demonstrate your willingness to help them. Once again, most people will appreciate that you thought of them.

Connect others

By putting other people in touch and helping them to broaden their own networks, you are expanding the realm of people that they can, in turn, put you in touch with. They will also remember the favor and return it one day.

Help others succeed

If it pays to know people in high places, then help others attain these high places, so that you can know them.

If you stay connected on a regular basis, *people will start to come to you as a source of information.* People will say, *"Call Jane — she knows everyone."* Or, *"Call Bob, he always knows what people are up to."* When you've achieved and maintained this level of connection with others, your calls to them will seem far less of an imposition than they might be if you hadn't made these ongoing efforts to stay connected.

STEP 4

Access Your Network

In order to achieve your career goals, or find the next great job, you need to be able to access your network. This means tapping into the collective resources and knowledge that other people in your network (and the people in their networks) have that could potentially be helpful to you. Accessing your network inherently requires you to ask people for things — information, introductions, advice, etc. The next section looks at this key activity of making requests in greater depth.

Making Requests

During a job search or career transition, and more specifically when we network, an important skill that we use — and often don't even know we are using — is the skill of making requests. When it is done well, we receive the information, introductions, and opportunities that we desire in a way that is respectful of others and builds relationships. When it is done poorly, we offend people, run into one dead end after another, and get increasingly frustrated.

TYPES OF REQUESTS

You make a request because you want something and, in doing so, you solicit future action from another person. There are many types of requests. Some examples include:

- Information about an industry
- Information about an organization, sector, or role
- Understanding the other person's own career path
- Honest feedback
- Help with brainstorming
- Additional connections or introductions
- Another meeting
- A personal recommendation

When making a request, you need to be very clear and specific. In addition, you need to assess the ability of the other person to fulfill the request:

- Do they have the time, ability, and resources to fulfill the request?
- Are they sincere and responsible in the commitments and promises that they make?

If you cannot answer yes to the questions above, you need to either reframe your request or move on.

COMMON MISTAKES IN MAKING REQUESTS

Not Making Requests

Very often, we don't make requests because we assume the answer will be no or fear that asking things of others shows weakness, is an imposition, or is manipulative in some way. For some, it is a sense of pride or self-reliance that keeps them from making requests of others, which is why it can feel more uncomfortable to make requests the more senior you get. You need to remember that *everyone* makes requests, including CEOs and executive directors (who make a lot of them). A "no" is not a rejection of you, it is simply a no to the request. When a request is denied, you can at least take comfort in the fact that someone is willing to be straight with you and that you can redirect your efforts toward more promising avenues.

Making Vague or Unclear Requests

Requests must be precise and detailed. The more specific they are, the easier it is for someone to help you. Often, people make unclear requests because they don't take the time to think through what they really want. Notice the difference between: *"Could you help me find a job in non-profit?"* and *"Do you know anyone with good knowledge of the Clinton Foundation?"* Which request is clearer about the help needed and what the other person is saying yes or no to?

Making Requests

COMMON MISTAKES IN MAKING REQUESTS

Not Paying Attention to the Tone of the Requests

Requests that sound desperate or demanding leave people feeling anxious, attacked, or manipulated into saying yes. As a result, the tone of your request or the word choice used can have a more negative impact than the request itself. You want your request to be confident (you've done your homework and believe that this is something the person can say yes to), somewhat tentative (recognizing that they may not be able to help at this time), and sincere (demonstrating your appreciation and willingness to reciprocate).

Neglecting Relationships and Reciprocity

Often, when we get consumed with our own needs, we think about requests as one-time or transactional events and become focused on getting what we want, rather than seeing this interaction as an exchange in a much bigger relationship. To build the relationship through your request, always ask: "*How can I make it easy for you to fulfill this request?*" and "*How can I help you?*"

Don't assume that because you are looking for a job, you are not in a position to help others. At a minimum, you can offer your gratitude, which is often all that people who are in a position to help want. Showing gratitude is imperative and goes a long way.

Beyond your sincere appreciation, you may be able to offer others useful information (for example, where to stay when on vacation in Costa Rica or who just got hired as a VP of strategy at your prior employer), resources (such as a valuable industry report you just delivered at a conference), or you may even give them something less tangible without knowing it (such as reinforcement of their self-concept of being an industry expert or of being well-networked).

Finally, you also open the door for them to come back to you when they are looking for assistance or for their next position by saying, "*Please don't hesitate to let me know if I can ever be helpful to you.*"

Cold and Warm Introductions

COLD INTRODUCTIONS

Cold introductions, or cold calls, are the often-dreaded phone calls or emails to individuals with whom you have no prior contact or connection. Ideally, you want to convert a cold call into a warm call by asking others for introductions. Always ask for introductions before jumping in to make the cold call. You can check LinkedIn to see if you have any contacts in common who could possibly introduce you. The extra effort may very well pay off and connect you directly to the hiring manager or recruiter (read: decision maker), and fast-track your application. However, sometimes after much effort to obtain an introduction, you cannot find a link to the person you would like to contact and a cold call may be necessary.

While cold calls are not the ideal way into an organization, they *do* work at times, and so should not be abandoned altogether. Below are some tips when making cold introductions:

- Start with a natural affinity group — your university alumni population or an industry association
- Leverage community leadership positions to reach out to industry professionals (e.g., contact marketing professionals in organizing a panel for a professional association conference)
- Be creative — sending an express envelope with a hard copy of your cover letter and resume may get the hiring manager's attention
- When sending an email, write "Introduction" in the subject header and make your message brief (no more than three short paragraphs)

Below is an example of a cold introductory email or letter:

To: Roberta Stevenson
From: Joe Jobseeker
Subject: Introduction

Dear Ms. Stevenson,

I came across your name on the company website/alumni database and am writing in reference to learning more about apparel industry careers and would also like to learn about American Apparel, in particular. I have a background in brand management in the consumer packaged goods sector, with over five years of experience at Clorox. I am currently exploring opportunities to leverage this experience in the apparel industry.

I am writing to see if it is possible to speak with you, briefly, to learn more about your company and solicit your valuable advice on how to build a career in the apparel industry. Please let me know some days/times that might work for you to talk in the weeks ahead.

I have also attached my resume, so that you may have a better idea of my background.

Best regards,

Joe Jobseeker

Cold and Warm Introductions

WARM INTRODUCTIONS

The same general approach is used when making a warm introduction. As with a cold introduction, we recommend that your first point of contact be an email to introduce yourself. When sending this e-mail, write *"Referred by James Lopez"* in the subject header so that the recipient will recognize the name and be more likely to open the email, read it and, most importantly, respond to it. Re-iterate, in the first sentence, the name of the referring individual.

Below is a modified version of the cold call letter or email adapted for a warm introduction.

> To: Roberta Stevenson
> From: Joe Jobseeker
> Subject: Referred by James Lopez
>
> Dear Ms. Stevenson,
>
> James Lopez, a former colleague of mine at Clorox, recommended that I contact you. I am a currently exploring potential careers in the apparel industry and am interested in learning more about your company, American Apparel. I have a strong background in consumer packaged goods and am looking for opportunities to leverage my brand management experience in the apparel industry.
>
> I am writing to see if it is possible to speak with you briefly to learn more about your company and solicit your valuable advice on how to build a career in the apparel industry. Please let me know some days/times that might work for you to talk in the weeks ahead.
>
> I have also attached my resume, so that you may have a better idea of my background. I look forward to speaking with you soon.
>
> Best regards,
>
> Joe Jobseeker

Cold and Warm Introductions

WARM INTRODUCTIONS

Requesting an Email Introduction

When asking others for an introduction, you want to make it as easy as possible for them. It can be helpful to draft a short email for your contact so they can use it to make the introduction. Always ask them to cc: you on their email introduction, as it will not only allow you to know the email has been sent, but it will also allow their contact to more easily respond directly to you and will allow you to directly reach out to them. Further, it will allow your contact to step aside as you continue the email exchange with the person to whom they've introduced you.

Below is a sample email to send when requesting an email introduction:

To: James Lopez
From: Joe Jobseeker
Subject: Request for Introduction

Hi James,

As you know, I'm exploring new opportunities in apparel and I was hoping you would be willing to introduce me to your contact at American Apparel, Roberta Stevenson. I've taken the liberty of drafting a description of me and what I'm looking for below to facilitate the process. It would be great if you could copy me on your email so I can follow up with her directly once you've made the introduction. I really appreciate your support. Please let me know if I can be of help to you in any way.

Best,
James

I am exploring a move into the apparel industry and am a big fan of American Apparel, both from a business and consumer perspective and have been impressed by how the company has developed. I am interested in learning more about the company and your contact's experiences.

A little about my background:

- I'm currently a brand manager at Clorox (5+ years' experience in packaged goods, including a successful new product launch)
- Prior to business school, I worked for 3 years in management consulting on a variety of projects including developing international growth strategies, customer strategy and marketing, and business performance optimization

I've attached a copy of my resume, which has more detail on my background.

Cold and Warm Introductions

WARM INTRODUCTIONS

Note that most people will prefer to ask their contact first if they'd be willing to talk with you before making the introduction. Below is the email your contact might send to their friend or colleague prior to making the introduction.

> To: Roberta Stevenson
> From: James Lopez
> Subject: Introduction
>
> Hi Roberta,
>
> I hope all is well with you. It was great to see you at the alumni event the other week.
>
> I am writing to ask a favor for a former colleague of mine, Joe Jobseeker. Joe is exploring a move into the apparel industry. He told me he's a big fan of American Apparel, both from a consumer and business perspective, and has been impressed by the way it's developed. He is interested in learning more about the company and your experiences. Would you be willing to chat with him briefly? If so, please let me know the best way for him to contact you. If it's not a good time for you, I understand.
>
> I also think you would enjoy meeting him as he's clearly passionate about this area, and is very capable. A quick bit about him:
>
> - He's currently a brand manager at Clorox (5+ years' experience in packaged goods, including a successful new product launch)
> - Prior to business school, he worked for 3 years in management consulting on a variety of projects including developing international growth strategies, customer strategy and marketing, and business performance optimization
>
> I've attached his resume, which has more detail on his background.
>
> Let me know if you are up for talking to him, and of course, please let me know if I can do anything for you!
>
> Warm regards,
> James

Cold and Warm Introductions

WARM INTRODUCTIONS

Assuming, in this example, Roberta Stevenson agrees to speak with Joe Jobseeker, James Lopez would send the email introduction to both parties. Your reply to the email introduction might look like the following:

> To: Roberta Stevenson, James Lopez
> From: Joe Jobseeker
> Subject: Introduction
>
> James, thanks for the introduction!
>
> Roberta, it's nice to meet you via email. I'd love to schedule some time with you to learn more about American Apparel and the apparel industry in general. I work nearby, so perhaps we can meet for coffee at your convenience? Please let me know some days / times that work for you in the weeks ahead.
>
> Best regards,
>
> Joe

Cold and Warm Introductions

CLOSING THE LOOP

After receiving an introduction and meeting your contact's friend, colleague, or acquaintance, it's important to circle back with your contact to close the loop. This entails giving an update on your interaction with the person to whom he introduced you and thanking him again for making the connection. Continuing from the prior example, this might look like the following via email:

> To: James Lopez
> From: Joe Jobseeker
> Subject: Introduction to Roberta Stevenson
>
> James,
>
> I hope you are doing well. I wanted to thank you again for the introduction to Roberta Stevenson at American Apparel and update you to let you know that I met with Roberta yesterday. It was very helpful to hear more about her experience at American Apparel and get her perspectives on where the company and industry are headed and areas where there might be opportunities within her company. She has also offered to connect me with a few more people internally, so I will let you know how that goes.
>
> Again, I am very appreciative of your introduction. Please don't hesitate to let me know if I can ever be of help to you in any way.
>
> All the best,
>
> Joe

Cold and Warm Introductions

CLOSING THE LOOP

Of course, you will want to send the person who met with you (Roberta Stevenson, in this example) a thank-you within 24 hours. The email below illustrates an appropriate thank-you email for this example.

> To: Roberta Stevenson
> From: Joe Jobseeker
> Subject: Thank you
>
> Roberta,
>
> Thank you so much for taking the time to meet with me today. It was really helpful to learn more about American Apparel and your experience working at the company, which reinforced my interest in both the company and the industry. I also really appreciated your perspective on what aspects of my background would be most valued at American Apparel. Finally, thank you for your kind offer to introduce me to some of your colleagues. Please let me know the best way to follow up on this. I look forward to staying in touch.
>
> All the best,
>
> Joe

Informational Interviews

Informational interviews are conversations with other people who are in a position to help you. Essentially, they are one type of networking meeting. They are a key element of the exploration and job search process, and are integral to any networking strategy. There are multiple benefits of conducting informational interviews:

- Learning about a new industry or function
- Learning about a specific role
- Learning about how others made a similar transition
- Making others aware of your goals
- Getting in front of potential hiring managers
- Demonstrating your initiative and motivation
- Letting people know you are committed to your job search
- Learning about upcoming opportunities
- Receiving feedback regarding your resume, background, and potential opportunities
- Tapping into new information, resources, and contacts
- Gaining valuable market intelligence and advice
- Expanding your network and gaining new introductions
- Maintaining momentum in your job search
- Positioning yourself to people in your target industry or function
- Getting unstuck!

Types of Informational Interviews

There are two types of informational interviews. The first type is *purely informational,* with the purpose of learning about a new area to which you have had limited or no prior exposure, and to gain feedback about your suitability for that position or career. This type of informational interview is good for those who currently have no clear or defined direction. In this type of informational interview, you are just collecting information, approaching the conversation with the curiosity of a journalist or a researcher. While you are not actively positioning yourself (at the moment) as a candidate, you are still being evaluated — remember, an informational interview is still an interview!

The second type of informational interview uses a *consultative sales approach.* This type of interview is more appropriate for those who have a clearer or well-defined direction. In addition to learning and collecting information as in the above-described informational interview, the goal is to find available job opportunities. Thus, this meeting is used to position yourself, to identify opportunities for you to make a contribution and to meet decision makers in the organization. Many people are able to use this type of informational interview to create a new opportunity that didn't previously exist. Just as a consultant would do with a client, individuals conducting this type of informational interview help the hiring manager identify existing business problems and, when appropriate, present their competencies and experience as a potential business solution.

Informational Interviews

Who should you ask for an informational interview? The lists below may spark ideas of people you could talk to and places where you can learn about people who would be helpful to meet.

People

Co-workers
Family members
Friends
Friends of friends
Mentors
Teachers/professors
Members/leaders of alumni associations
Past employers/colleagues
Community organization members
Classmates
Stock/industry analysts
Venture capitalists/investors

Business associates
Doctors/lawyers/dentists/bankers
Merchants
Members of place of worship
Club members
Neighbors
Consultants
Seminar/conference participants
Speakers
Authors
Members of school community
Industry association members/leaders

Places

Professional organizations
Career centers, schools
Government offices

Chamber of Commerce
Executive search firms
Employment offices

Written and On-line Materials

Trade publications
Local business publications
Career books
Book of lists
Business journals/periodicals
Blogs

Social networking sites (e.g. LinkedIn)
Annual reports
Articles/newspapers
Business directories
Job postings
Industry research reports

Informational Interviews

Below are some questions to help you think about where (and with whom) to conduct informational interviews:

In which industries do you want to conduct informational interviews?
....
....

In what organizations do you want to conduct informational interviews?
....
....

Who do you know directly at these organizations that you can contact?
....
....

Who can you ask for introductions?
....
....

Which informational interviews are purely informational?
....
....

Which informational interviews are aimed at finding a specific opportunity?
....
....

How many informational interviews will you conduct in the next month and with whom?
....
....
....
....
....
....

Informational Interviews

BASIC STRUCTURE

A key way to make a good impression in an informational interview is to be organized. While informational interviews may, at times, be relaxed, that doesn't mean they should lack direction. You should have a clear purpose or sense of how you'd like to use the other person's time and set the basic agenda or structure of the conversation. In doing so, the other person who is taking time out of his busy schedule feels like you have used his time well and that he was actually able to be of assistance. As a result, he will be more inspired to be of further assistance to you.

The basic structure of the informational interview is:

1) **Thank the other person for taking the time to talk to you and confirm how much time you have with him**
   "Thank you so much for taking the time to meet with me today. I first want to confirm how much time you have so I can be sure to wrap up on time....We have half an hour — terrific."

2) **Introduce yourself using your positioning statement**
   "I've been a management consultant for the last five years, where I specialized in helping organizations improve operational effectiveness. What I enjoyed most was working with organizations that had a social impact."

3) **Explain why you wanted to meet with them or what you are looking for**
   "Given my interests, I'm investigating whether philanthropy would be a good sector in which to work, so I'd like to learn more about this area, as well as what it's like to work at the Gates Foundation."

4) **State why you'd like to meet with them in particular**
   "Greg also said you were able to successfully transition to the non-profit world from management consulting. I'd love to learn more about how you made this transition and any advice that you may have based on your experience making this change."

5) **Focus your questions first on the other person, their experience, insights, points of view, etc.**
   "What were some of the challenges you faced in entering philanthropy? What skills do you draw on most from your management consulting days in your current job?...."

6) **Share in greater depth your background and experience, particularly, where relevant to the job, company, or industry you are exploring**
   "One project that I worked on involved evaluating our client's Corporate Social Responsibility function and suggesting to them ways they could broaden their impact to a global level...I found that I was really energized by their focus on making a social impact, particularly on a global scale. This also involved benchmarking what other companies' CSR functions were doing..."

7) **Ask for feedback on your suitability for that job, company, or industry — strengths you should leverage, as well as perceived gaps and how you might bridge those gaps**
   "Based on my background and experience, where would you see me contributing most to an organization, such as the Gates Foundation — or some other foundation? What do you see as my strengths and experience that I should be emphasizing? What do you see as gaps in my experience that might present a challenge in making this type of transition to the world of philanthropy? What would you suggest that I do to help bridge those gaps to be seen as a more attractive candidate to foundations?"

8) **Ask for further introductions**
   "To the extent that you know of other people that would be helpful for me to talk to, I'd love to meet them. Does anyone come to mind?"

Informational Interviews

BASIC STRUCTURE

9) Thank them for their time and ask to stay in touch

"Thank you so much for your time today, I really appreciate it. I'd also like to stay in touch with you. Would it be ok if I reconnected with you in a few months to give you an update on how things are going or ask any additional questions?"

While each informational interview will be somewhat unique and may vary in its objective, following the above basic structure will be a good start. Remember that an informational interview is still an interview, so you'll want to make a good impression!

SAMPLE QUESTIONS

The questions listed below can be used effectively to learn about specific roles, careers, and organizations. If you use them and tailor them to each situation, you will be able to successfully increase your knowledge, target those opportunities appropriate to you, and build your network.

In informational interviews, stress the positive and remember, it is not entirely about you — it is about the person you are interviewing and his or her organization or industry. However, there may be appropriate openings to discuss your experiences and skills and how they apply to the industry or function being discussed. Get people to talk about what they enjoy doing, what they've been good at, and the successes they've enjoyed before focusing on the more challenging job aspects.

There are four main areas of focus for your questions. They are:

1. The Person You Are Interviewing
- How did you come to be doing _____?
- What aspect of your background best prepared you for this role?
- How do you spend a typical day?
- What keeps you up at night?
- What kinds of people do you interact with? Have access to?
- What are your typical work hours?
- What skills do you use that make you good at what you do?
- What skills don't you use as often?
- What would you really like to get done that you haven't — because of choice or lack of time?

2. The Job
- What are your most recent successes in your job?
- What do you enjoy about your work?
- What do you like least about the job?
- What do you delegate to subordinates?
- What does your boss delegate to you?
- What are your top three priorities?
- What parts of your job are the most challenging?
- What else would you like to be doing in your job?
- What are the criteria for success in your job?
- What are the salary ranges for this type of work?

Informational Interviews

SAMPLE QUESTIONS

3. The Organization
- How many years do people typically stay in the job? With this organization?
- How would you describe the culture?
- How are goals set and measured? How often?
- What type of training or management development is available?
- What is the feedback mechanism, frequency, source, and approach?
- What types of people do well here?
- What is the profile of the ideal person that you would hire for your job? For this department?
- What are possible career paths in this department/organization?
- What are the trends/projections for this organization? This industry?
- What competitors do you particularly admire? Why?
- How is success rewarded?

4. You
- Given my background, what skills and experience do I have that are applicable?
- Where are there gaps or areas of concern? How do you recommend that I address these?
- What journals/magazines/blogs should I read?
- What networking organizations and associations should I join?
- What classes would be most useful in preparing for this career?
- What else would you recommend to learn more about this industry/function?
- Given what you have learned in your career, what advice would you give me?
- What do you wish someone had told you before taking this job or entering this industry?
- Who else do you recommend I speak to? May I use your name?

Action Planning

Given the amount of work that goes into a job search, and the various elements involved, it is important to create an action plan. What goals would you like to have accomplished one month from now? What actions do you need to take to achieve those goals? What resources or support do you need? Draft a plan for the next month that you can commit to putting into action. You may then break down some of these goals and incorporate them into the *Momentum Matrix* on *pages 7–8*.

GOAL	ACTIONS	RESOURCES
Example: Secure interviews at one of my top five target companies	• Identify company contacts • Arrange at least 10 networking meetings • Research top five target companies	• Industry reports • Professional association membership • Company websites

Action Planning

The following questions may assist your planning and help to create momentum in your search:

What goals would you like to have accomplished one month from now?

What might prevent you from accomplishing those goals?

How much time will you devote (per day, per week) to this pursuit?

What are the interim steps?

What more do you need to know?

Who can you talk to?

What skills do you need to develop and how can you develop them?

What support do you need and from whom?

How will you celebrate when you achieve your key milestones?

PART 4

Job Search Execution

Cover Letters

Cover letters are used to introduce yourself to a hiring manager, a networking contact, or an informational interview prospect, and may or may not involve a referral. Most cover letters are now done by email, but some are still written and presented the old-fashioned way — on paper.

ELEMENTS

There are three elements of the cover letter:

1. Introduce yourself and explain the purpose of writing

In this section you may:

- Reference your contact. If the cover letter is sent by email, and it is a warm contact (i.e., you were referred by someone), put *"Referred by John Doe"* in the subject header so that the recipient is more likely to open, read, and respond to your email. Your opening line should then reiterate *"John Doe suggested that I contact you...."* If it is a cold contact (where there is no referral involved), you can put *"Introduction"* in the subject header, or *"Candidate for [position title]."*
- Briefly explain what you know about the company and why it is of interest to you.
- Describe how you could make a contribution by relating your most relevant accomplishments and experience to the position if you are writing regarding a specific job.

2. Describe your accomplishments concisely

Make it clear that you can do the job and would be a strong addition to the company. Make sure your accomplishments reflect the job requirements.

3. Close with a specific request

For example, ask to speak further with the recipient to learn about the industry/organization/job or discuss your qualifications.

MORE KEY POINTS

In addition, your cover letter should:

- Be addressed to the hiring manager or other key decision maker.
- Be concise — one page with no more than two to three brief paragraphs.
- Show your enthusiasm for the industry/organization/job.
- Include one to two relevant accomplishments.

With your first draft, be sure to get feedback from a colleague or a friend on the clarity of your request and overall message and tone.

An example of a good cover letter is shown on the following page.

Cover Letters

SAMPLE COVER LETTER

To: Camila Ortiz
From: Alejandro Roth
Subject: Candidate for Senior Manager, Partner Marketing – Latin America Position

Dear Camila,

I am writing in reference to the Senior Manager, Partner Marketing – Latin America position at Netflix. I have been a Netflix customer for over 10 years and have been impressed by how the company has evolved. In addition, I believe that my background and experience make me a strong candidate for this position to help Netflix continue its growth globally.

I am bi-lingual and have extensive sales and marketing experience in Latin America. Specifically, I identified, pursued, and negotiated multiple partnerships in Latin America for Yahoo valued at approximately $10 million, and I have managed the full partnership lifecycle. In addition, while at Hispanic Global, I leveraged my project management skills to implement multiple sales and marketing programs in various countries and cultures, resulting in the successful acquisition of thousands of new customers.

I am attaching my resume so that you may see more about my background. I'd appreciate the opportunity to further discuss my qualifications. Please let me know if there is a good time for you to speak in the weeks ahead. I'm also happy to work with your assistant to find a mutually convenient time to talk.

Thank you in advance for your consideration.

Best regards,

Alejandro Roth
408-555-1212
alejandro.roth@yahoo.com

Resumes

Your resume (in addition to your LinkedIn profile) is your most important marketing document. Resume literally means *summary*. It is a *brief* written account of personal, educational, and professional qualifications and experience. It is not a laundry list of everything you have ever done. You will want to highlight the most relevant aspects of your experience and minimize, or even eliminate, that which is no longer relevant to your current career goals.

If you are a part-time or executive MBA student, your school likely has its own preferred format (typically limited to one page) for use in resume books and on-campus recruiting. Check with your Career Center and follow its standard format as instructed, as it is usually required to take advantage of on-campus recruiting opportunities.

If you are not currently in school or are conducting an independent job search, you may choose to use a different resume format, or use a two-page resume. Two-page resumes are perfectly acceptable, particularly if you have considerable experience. The pages that follow provide guidelines for such a resume.

Resumes

ANATOMY OF A RESUME

Heading
- Place name prominently in bold, using the largest size font on the page
- Include phone, email, and postal address in your contact information, using a smaller font than in the main body of the resume

Summary
- Describe your area of expertise in the first few words (i.e., Marketing Professional)
- Limit to three to five lines or bullets
- Don't use an objective statement

Experience

Do:

- Focus on accomplishments — What was the result? Quantify these where possible
- Qualify results if unable to quantify (i.e., *"Received senior management approval for...."*)
- Use bullet format for these accomplishments
- Start each bullet with an action verb (*see page 162 for a list*)
- Be concise
- Emphasize skills that you want to continue to use and develop
- Use key words or phrases most applicable to your desired position or industry
- Devote more space to recent or most relevant work experience

Don't:

- Write in paragraphs — you will lose the reader's attention instantly
- Use passive statements (i.e., *"responsible for"*) — rephrase to active form
- Use excessive industry jargon
- Emphasize activities you don't enjoy
- Speak in the first person (i.e., *"I organized..."*)
- Devote too much space to work experience that is less relevant or over 15 years old
- Include months when listing dates if at an employer for more than one year
- Include a photo, birth date, or marital/family status typically found on international CVs

Education
- If not in school, include this section after the experience section. (If in school, and you are looking to make a career change, you may put Education before Experience)
- Include *relevant* recent clubs and activities
- List most important awards
- Omit dates of prior degrees (as they are not obligatory) if you are concerned about potential age discrimination
- Include any technical training or continuing education

Resumes

ANATOMY OF A RESUME

Additional information
- Note any special certifications (i.e., CFA, CPA, Series 7, etc.)
- Include *relevant* foreign language proficiencies
- Include community and professional affiliations and any leadership positions
- Include other awards, publications, patents, speaking engagements, etc.
- Include unique or interesting accomplishments or interests (i.e., climbed Mt. McKinley, finished NY Marathon, avid mountain biker). This shows your personality and is a way to potentially connect with a hiring manager or recruiter!
- List work authorization or security clearances, if relevant

RESUME TIPS

Below are some additional tactical suggestions to make your resume even better. You may feel that some suggestions are more helpful than others. In the end, it is *your* document — you are the one who must feel comfortable that your resume accurately reflects your accomplishments and career potential.

- Make it aesthetically pleasing — use white space and margins
- Use Times New Roman or Arial font
- Do not use font sizes below 10 point
- Explain prolonged gaps (i.e., 2010–2013, primary caregiver for child or elderly parent)
- Limit your resume to two pages maximum (unless you have a separate deal sheet, publications list, or lengthy patent list attached as an addendum)
- Make sensible page breaks so the information flows well and is easy to follow
- Adjust formatting or content to fill at least two-thirds of the second page to make it visually appealing, if using two pages
- Label "Page 1 of 2" and "Page 2 of 2" in the footer
- Repeat name and phone number on second page, in case pages are separated
- Let go of your "stuff" (the roles and accomplishments that are no longer relevant)
- Don't list "References available upon request" since this is obvious
- Always spellcheck
- Use a limited number of versions — too many will be confusing for you to manage
- Save as "firstname lastname resume.doc" to make it easier for recruiters to find
- Don't save file with "consulting resume" in the title. This implies you have other versions and may not be focused
- Save as a pdf file to preserve formatting when emailing others your resume

When Drafting Your Resume
- Look at old performance reviews
- Speak with old bosses and colleagues to refresh your memory of your accomplishments
- Get feedback from others who may catch mistakes or make helpful suggestions

Most Importantly
- Don't get "analysis paralysis" and spend an excessive amount of time on this document; it is more important to get out and meet people than to make your resume perfect
- If you make it hard to read...*it won't be read!*

Resumes

RESUME FORMATS

There are various resume formats and styles. Each resume format is best used under certain circumstances. Below is a description of these resume formats and when each is most or least helpful.

Chronological Resume
- Lists work history in reverse chronological order (starts with most recent job)
- Clearly ties accomplishments to specific jobs, organizations, and time frames

Most helpful when:
- Your career history shows steady or significant growth and development
- You are looking to stay in your current field, or a field closely tied to your experience
- Your previous employers have been prestigious

Least helpful when:
- You are changing careers
- Your new career goals are dramatically different from your past experience
- Your work history is erratic or you have changed employers frequently
- You have been absent from the job market for an extended period of time

Functional Resume
- Designed to emphasize the candidate's competencies and qualifications
- Puts less emphasis on employers and specific dates
- Is not recognized by all recruiters or hiring managers who may prefer a chronological format

Most helpful when:
- Your career goal is very different from your past experience
- You want to emphasize competencies not used in your most recent work experience
- You have many, diverse work experiences with no common theme
- You are entering the job market after an extended absence

Least helpful when:
- Your past employers have been prestigious
- You want to highlight your career growth in a particular field

Combined Format
- Presents work experience chronologically
- Breaks out experience within each job or employer under functional areas

The following pages show examples of each of the above resume formats.

Resumes

CHRONOLOGICAL RESUME

JAMES WALSH
222 Green Street • San Francisco, CA 94123
(415) 555-1234
JamesWalsh@yahoo.com

SUMMARY

Strategy professional with strong quantitative and team skills. Track record in investment analysis and identifying operational efficiencies. Proven ability to operate in high stress environments.

EXPERIENCE

2012–Present   **BAIN & COMPANY**   San Francisco, CA
Consultant

Conducted and articulated detailed, data-driven strategic analysis for clients in the air transportation, semiconductor, private equity, and consumer packaged goods industries.
- Created financial return on investment model to help assess new opportunities for semiconductor client. Resulted in client adoption of model and methodology for assessing future opportunities and overhaul of company's investment process.
- Identified over $60M in short-term operational efficiency savings in the post-merger integration of 2 cargo airline route networks.
- Presented pricing analysis findings to CEO in the express package delivery industry. Analysis dramatically changed pricing policy and accelerated launch of 2 product lines, thereby improving company's competitive position.,
- Consistently recognized internally and by client senior management for developing realistic solutions to problems in several functional areas including pricing, organization design, and logistics.
- Captained the annual United Way office-fund drive, coordinating 20 office volunteers producing office-wide events; achieved the highest per capita and participation rate among firms in the Bay Area.

2007–2010   **HEADQUARTERS, SUBMARINE FORCE, U.S. PACIFIC FLEET**   Pearl Harbor, HI
Special Security Officer and Command Center Watch Officer

Oversaw security for Defense Top Secret information. Managed team of 6 Navy staff located around the Pacific Rim.
- Awarded Navy Commendation Medal.
- Trained 25 submarine crews to properly handle Top Secret information while conducting missions vital to national security. Managed security clearances for 850 sailors.
- Analyzed security and conducted initial certification of Top Secret computer network. Implemented electronic message routing and saved 3800 man-hours per year.
- Ranked consistently in top 10% of peers.
- Spearheaded initial response for operations, communications, and crisis situations involving submarines in the Pacific and Indian Oceans and Persian Gulf. Supervised team of 20 people.

2005–2006   **USS KAMEHAMEHA, FAST ATTACK NUCLEAR SUBMARINE**   Pearl Harbor, HI
Operations and Nuclear Engineering Watch Officer and Division Officer

Directed ship navigation and engineering in stressful, high traffic environments. Supervised a 10-sailor team operating a nuclear power plant. Qualified Naval Nuclear Chief Engineer by Department of Energy.
- Awarded 2 Navy Achievement Medals.
- Developed an internal Quality Assurance surveillance system, restructured the training program, and improved maintenance procedures. Reduced deficiency comments on external audit by 65%.

EDUCATION

2010–2012   **TUCK SCHOOL OF BUSINESS AT DARTMOUTH**   Hanover, NH
Master of Business Administration

2004–2005   **NAVAL NUCLEAR POWER SCHOOL**   Orlando, FL
Advanced coursework in Nuclear Engineering; Nuclear Propulsion Plant Supervisor certification.

2000–2004   **UNITED STATES NAVAL ACADEMY**   Annapolis, MD
Bachelor of Science degree in Mathematics with Honors; graduated Cum Laude, top 15% of class.

OTHER

Active private pilot. Enjoy traveling, cycling, weightlifting, and competitive swimming. Held Top Secret security clearance.

Resumes

COMBINED FORMAT – EXAMPLE 1

Ravi Desai
777 6th Street, Menlo Park, CA 94025 • 650-333-4444 • Ravi@Desai.com

Summary:
Experienced consumer marketing manager with proven ability in marketing billion-dollar consumer high tech brands. International experience working in Europe and South America. Recognized for excellent communication skills and ability to lead large, cross-functional teams. Results oriented, highly disciplined, and strong team player.

Experience:

2010–Present   **INTEL CORPORATION**   Santa Clara, CA
Corporate Marketing Group

Worldwide Consumer Marketing Manager (2010–Present)
Lead worldwide cross-functional teams in the development of consumer campaign marketing plans to create awareness and demand for Intel's premium brands: Intel® Centrino™ mobile technology and Pentium® 4 processor. Rank consistently in top quartile of peer group.
Intel Centrino Mobile Technology (CMT) Brand:
- **Strategy:** Drove development process of consumer marketing and channel strategy for the Intel Centrino mobile technology product launch, Intel's largest product launch in 10+ years.
- **Messaging:** Developed end user messaging in collaboration with product marketing division and selected and managed agency to develop copy for use across retail, event collateral and the Intel Inside® Program. Campaign recognized by top management to be Intel's most successful campaign.
- **Program Management:** Created vision and received executive management buy-in for a national series of events targeting professional women to generate excitement for wireless computing and CMT. Events met or exceeded attendance goals and 85%+ of attendees stated they were more motivated to get wireless after attending event.
- **International:** Selected for a three-month assignment in Munich, Germany, to manage European messaging project including qualitative research resulting in consistent European-wide messages. Owned Intel-Sony co-marketing budget of $5 million and program definition for Germany, UK, and France.

Program Manager, Intel Latin America (2010)   Buenos Aires, Argentina
- Led redesign project for *Intel.com Latin America*, including management of marcom agency in Brazil, localization of content and coordination with team in U.S.
- Served as client manager for more than 35 Intel partners participating in the *Buenos Aires Intel® eBusiness Forum*.

2006–2010   **THE WEBER GROUP**   Palo Alto, CA
High-tech public relations agency owned by McCann-Erickson Worldgroup

Assistant Account Executive
- Developed press releases for new product launches for clients such as Xerox New Enterprises, Pervasive Software and Computer Curriculum Corporation (CCC).
- Secured 40% increase in client's budget as result of team's successful media engagements.

Education:

2002–2006   **UNIVERSITY OF VIRGINIA**   Charlottesville, VA
BA Degree in English Language and Literature; Dean's List
Studied two semesters in Perú and Argentina

Additional: Spanish fluency (speaking, reading, writing); Enjoy skiing, cooking, Latin dance and travel; Board Member of *The Indus Entrepreneurs*, Volunteer English teacher.

COMBINED FORMAT – EXAMPLE 2

SARAH RUSSELL

66 Fenway Drive 917-555-1212
Stamford, CT 06903 srussell@gmail.com

SUMMARY
Seasoned media executive with broad experience leading worldwide distribution of television content and digital media assets for major global brands. Respected, thoughtful communicator. Proven ability to execute strategic vision by leading teams of marketing, programming, licensing, and distribution executives in the U.S. and abroad. Passionate problem solver and business builder, with excellent track record of creating new brands/products, and strategic partnerships, while operating businesses of significant scale.

A+E NETWORKS, LLC	New York, N.Y.	2004 – present
EVP, General Manager, Enterprises		2009-present
SVP, Enterprises		2006-2009
VP, General Manager Consumer Products		2004-2005

Business Development
- Led team of 500 staff, delivering double-digit annual growth for nine consecutive years.
- Formed seven joint operating channel ventures, with combined market capitalization $1.2 billion.
- Served as senior board member of the operating JVs, managing the growth in each region.
- Created licensing and sales teams for content syndication and digital distribution, achieving $50 million in revenues in this business segment.
- Developed global licensing group for consumer product extensions of hit shows, delivering triple digit growth over the last three years.
- Built ongoing profitable digital partnerships, including Apple, Netflix, Amazon, and Microsoft.
- Created the U.S. digital media practice, launching HISTORY.com 2.0.

International
- Built channels and content syndication business growing from $34 million to $425 million.
- Managed JV Teams in Latin America, Europe, and Asia, achieving #1,2 or 3 channel rank status.
- Led the creation of a new global brand, Crime & Investigation, in 200 million homes worldwide.
- Led team that created "web in a box" award-winning companion TV websites.
- Developed 11,000-hour catalog content syndication business, growing to $45 million in 2012.

Consumer Products
- Built home entertainment business, tripling revenues to $75 million.
- Developed brand licensing business, working with talent from hit shows to create new incremental revenue streams across retail, services, and entertainment sectors.
- Created the History Magazine club, membership of more than 275,000 paid subscribers.
- Negotiated a landmark Education partnership for HISTORY and Houghton Mifflin Harcourt, resulting in a new 21st century social studies digital curriculum, and licensing fees of $40 million.
- Ramped up e-commerce business to $12 million, expanded product to fan gear for hit shows.

Digital Media & Internet
- Defined mission and built team of 75 to execute strategic goals.
- Produced initial 10,000 short-form content clips to fuel traffic growth.
- Managed the growth and development of all A+E Networks web sites and mobile apps.
- Developed and launched HISTORY.com 2.0 driving unique visitors to more than five million and average time spent to ten minutes.
- Acquired Genealogy.com, a subscription and transaction search site for family history, and ultimately sold to rollup competitor MyFamily.com.

Page 1 of 2

COMBINED FORMAT – EXAMPLE 2

SARAH RUSSELL   917-555-1212   Page 2 of 2

THINGS REMEMBERED   Cleveland, Ohio   2003-2004
SVP, General Merchandise Manager

- Doubled profitability of this 800-store gift company in 18 months.
- Designed and launched first e-commerce website; became #1 store in the chain.
- Upgraded product assortment, sourcing 75% from Taipei, Seoul, Bangkok, and Guan Dong.
- Created new store prototype driving 30% store growth in new "A" concept stores.

3SIXTY, INC   New York, New York   2000-2002
Chief Operating Officer

- Raised "A" round financing of $20 million for children's fantasy sports 50-store/ e-commerce start-up.
- Built and executed operating plan, and hired corporate staff.
- Developed and opened prototype headquarters store as proof of concept.

BARNES & NOBLE, LLC   New York, New York   1997-1999
VP, General Merchandise Manager

- General Manager of B&N College Division for merchandising and marketing. Achieved 20% YOY growth, reaching $250 million annual sales.
- Designed and built first ever B&N university café-style campus bookstores.
- Launched over 200 university websites to support bookstore revenues and services.
- Built relationships with business affairs officials at top institutions leading to contracts at Harvard, Yale, University of Chicago, and Columbia University.

EDUCATION

MBA   UCLA Anderson School of Management, Los Angeles, California
BS   Cornell University, Ithaca, New York

PROFESSIONAL AFFILIATIONS

International Academy of Television
Executive Committee and Board member

Creative Good
Executive Council member for media and entertainment

CablePac
Member

Highschoolbattles.com
Advisor/mentor

Lean Launch Ventures, LLC
Advisor/mentor

Viagogo.com
Investor

OTHER

Basketball player, golfer, novice chef

FUNCTIONAL RESUME

JAIME HERNANDEZ

2000 Smith Avenue
Palo Alto, California 94111

650.222.5555
jaime@yahoo.com

SUMMARY

General Manager with broad experience in business development, marketing strategy, team management, financial functions, and international operations. Excellent problem solving and communication skills, strong ability to conceptualize and execute initiatives requiring effective decision making, project management, teamwork, and implementation of integrated solutions. Known for proven leadership and ability to build and expand business opportunities.

GENERAL MANAGEMENT CAREER HIGHLIGHTS

ADMINISTRATION
- Managed recruiting, on-boarding, and staffing of a 400-person call center.
- Led 20 FTE business development unit generating $5 million in revenues.
- Administered web and desktop applications for 6,000 call center users. Managed 20 FTEs.
- Managed database marketing unit analyzing client relationships and product profitability.

TECHNOLOGY APPLICATIONS
- Installed new e-mail system increasing internal capacity to 3,000 simultaneous users.
- Designed and implemented $6 million IPO system integrating web, VRU, and live channels.
- Installed $2 million intelligent call routing system, improving response time by 10%.
- Implemented Spanish and Chinese VRU services for 25,000 clients.

FINANCE AND ANALYSIS
- Managed $350 million operating budget as financial controller for 3,500 FTE organization.
- Installed internal financial controls resulting in $10 million cost reduction.
- Developed forecasting models for key business metrics and monitored variances.
- Collaborated in Schwab's initial public offering, performing financial valuation.

MARKETING
- Formulated positioning and marketing strategies for clients with $100k+ in assets.
- Planned and executed affinity programs for top 100,000 affluent clients.
- Increased affluent client retention by 3% and assets under management by 5%.
- Administered referral program with independent investment managers capturing $2 billion.

OPERATIONS
- Administered call center traffic operation supporting 120,000 daily calls.
- Implemented call routing service for top 100,000 clients reducing response time by 10 seconds.
- Distributed 12 IPOs among Schwab's best clients. Distributed over 1 million shares.
- Streamlined call center phone operations leading to 5% increase in capacity utilization.

INTERNATIONAL
- Launched business development unit targeting Hispanics. Managed staff of 20 FTEs.
- Opened offices in Miami and Puerto Rico. Captured 5,000 accounts and $250 million in assets.
- Developed ethnic marketing programs in Spanish and Chinese, attracting 10,000 new clients.
- Led US project liaison team integrating London branch into Schwab's operation.

Page 1 of 2

FUNCTIONAL RESUME

JAIME HERNANDEZ　　　　　　　　　　　　　　　　　　　　　　　　650.222.5555

WORK EXPERIENCE

CHARLES SCHWAB & CO., INC.　　　San Francisco, California　　　1995 – 2014

- SVP, Retail Client Services — Technology Solutions　　　2010 – 2014
- SVP, Retail Strategic Planning and Information　　　2005 – 2010
- VP, Retail Affluent Marketing　　　2001 – 2005
- VP, International Division　　　1996 – 2001
- VP, Market Research and Business Analysis　　　1995 – 1996

GRUPO ALFA　　　Monterrey, Mexico　　　1991 – 1993

- Strategic Planning Analyst

TECNOLOGICO DE MONTERREY　　　Monterrey, Mexico　　　1989 – 1990

- Full-time Instructor

EDUCATION

MBA, Stanford University, Stanford, California, 1995

BS, Chemical Engineering, M.I.T., Cambridge, MA 1988

Resumes

SPECIAL SITUATIONS

Career Re-entry

Individuals re-entering the workforce after an extended leave (e.g., to be a primary care giver for a child or parent) often face the question about what to do with the gap in their resumes. You can highlight volunteer positions you held during this time, whether they are for a charity or non-profit in which you have been involved or volunteer work you've done for your child's school or sports league. Focus on transferable competencies that will be attractive to a potential employer — these might include things like project management, fundraising, organization skills, etc.

Second Act Careers

As a large portion of the population approaches retirement age, there are a significant number of people who are not ready to retire — they want to continue to be engaged in the working world in some way, but are interested in pursuing something different than their primary career. They are looking for their second act. If this is the case for you, you might want to take a step back and think about the competencies that you are good at and have enjoyed using in your primary career. Breaking down your primary career experience into these functional categories can be a good way to show others what you can bring to the job.

Just as for any other resume, get feedback from others, but don't get 'analysis paralysis.' The most productive thing to do is to have a document that gives a good overview of your experience so you can get out and talk to people. Sample resumes that apply to each of these special situations are shown on the following pages.

Resumes

CAREER RE-ENTRY RESUME

Amy Connelly

3000 Ranch Road (512) 555-0022
Austin, TX 78610 aconnelly@gmail.com

SUMMARY

Successful project leader with broad experience in building and managing cross-functional teams. Proven track record in leading projects to achieve results on time and on budget. Strong ability to multi-task, engage key stakeholders, and influence without formal authority. Balances strategic thinking and attention to detail and works well in fast-paced environments. Excellent written and oral communication skills.

EXPERIENCE

Austin Library Foundation, 2006 – present Austin, TX
Campaign Co-chair, Board Member (2006–present)
President of the Board of Directors (2007–2010)

The Austin Library Foundation is a non-profit that spearheads fundraising campaigns for a modern, vibrant library system.

- Served as Chair of successful three-year, $5 million capital campaign
- Analyzed multiple sources of information to create prospect list for campaign
- Rebuilt board and brand after completion of first campaign
- Trained other board members in fundraising methods
- Led 12-member Board of Directors and two part-time employees
- Established strong partnerships with related non-profits and city departments
- Led selection committee for contractor to renovate older libraries

Renew Austin Libraries, 2006 Austin, TX
Chair of Campaign Committee

Renew Austin Libraries was a political campaign formed to pass a $65 million bond measure to rebuild three libraries. It succeeded where prior attempts to modernize the library system had failed.

- Designed strategy to raise public approval level four points to pass measure
- Implemented unprecedented level of fundraising and communication
- Managed over 100 volunteers using a three-tier structure
- Created focused monthly agendas for various committees and led weekly planning meetings
- Personally presented campaign position to dozens of audiences, including print and online media
- Wrote campaign materials and op-ed pieces that were published in *The Austin Chronicle*

CAREER RE-ENTRY RESUME

Oracle, 1995–2001 — Redwood Shores, CA
Member of Strategy Team, 2001

- Provided sales experience to consultants planning new Internet strategy
- Defined new market opportunities and potential solutions

Planning and Operations Manager, Worldwide Enterprise Sales, 1999–2000

- Served as Chief of Staff for this worldwide division
- Created and implemented communication plan for worldwide VP
- Worked with regional sales leaders to identify common sales issues and market opportunities
- Managed quarterly agendas for worldwide meetings
- Identified customer satisfaction issues for escalation and resolution

Sales Representative, 1997–1999

- Earned membership to President's Club
- Substantially exceeded annual sales targets
- Sold enterprise software to manufacturing customers
- Managed up to ten customer relationships at a time
- Identified cross-selling opportunities, resulting in significant additional sales
- Worked closely with technical consulting and configuration as well as post-sales service to ensure accurate orders and prompt resolution of all customer issues

Financial Analyst, Americas Sales, 1995–1997

- Analyzed and forecasted order revenue, discounts, and costs for sales managers
- Developed simple, integrated report for managers to understand their results
- Used multiple reporting systems to generate monthly financial reports
- Organized sales information for the district, area, and vertical/region managers and provided key metrics needed to manage their business and make decisions

United States House Budget Committee, 1992–1994 — Washington, DC
Analyst in Budget Review

Budget Review is a nonpartisan group that serves as the intermediary between members of Congress and the Congressional Budget Office.

- Prepared numerical and written analyses of multi-year budget proposals
- Wrote reports and other briefings for members of Congress, frequently under tight deadlines

EDUCATION

University of Texas at Austin
BA in Economics and History – Dean's Service Award
Certificate in Project Management

OTHER

Completed two triathlons. Fluent in Spanish.

SECOND ACT RESUME

SARAH BENSON

500 West 86th Street, New York, NY 10024
Phone: (646) 555-1212   Email: ssbenson@gmail.com

SUMMARY

Senior executive with solid finance/accounting background and strong business acumen. Proven track record in building teams and organizations. Passion for and deep experience in non-profit leadership. Dedicated volunteer serving underprivileged communities through active Board leadership. Strong history of developing deep and lasting client relationships. Ability to influence and connect with diverse constituencies as well as develop and execute organizational vision and strategic plans.

WORK EXPERIENCE

Benson & Morris LLC   New York, NY
Principal and Director   1986 - present

Firm Management/Administration
- Served as managing partner for 5 years
- Managed and coordinated all aspects of firm administration, including billing, human resources, and financial reporting
- Developed structure to admit, compensate and transition principals
- Coordinated annual budgets of up to $17M, as well as reporting and compliance for the firm
- Negotiated and reviewed all lease and building-related aspects of the business, realizing savings of up to $600,000

Marketing/Business Development
- Led firm growth from 10 professionals to over 90 professionals
- Created referral relationships which provided 15% annual growth in revenue
- Formulated marketing strategies that focused on industry niches, resulting in 10 to 20 new clients annually
- Secured and managed largest client of the firm, resulting in an increase in revenue of $700,000 annually for 10+ years

Finance and Analysis
- Oversaw the entire phase of compliance engagements and tax preparation for diverse clients; including non-profit organizations, real estate, wholesale distribution, logistics, professional services, healthcare, and high-net-worth individuals
- Negotiated the acquisition of numerous firms into the existing practice, dramatically increasing firm size and revenue
- Conceptualized creative tax planning ideas, such as repositioning assets that reduced tax bills and significantly increased owner's total after-tax income for high net worth individuals
- Assisted business clients in creating personal and estate tax plans to protect assets and assure adequate retirement income, including unified tax credit, insurance policies, and trusts
- Leveraged industry expertise in developing a plan that separated the business into two corporations for a contractor with business at risk of lawsuit, resulting in protection of hard-earned asset and prevention of a large tax bill

Client Service/Operations
- Leveraged a team of 90 professionals to service clients
- Coordinated and supervised annual audits and reviews of financial statements
- Developed new strategies to provide existing clients additional services

SECOND ACT RESUME

SARAH BENSON

Email: ssbenson@gmail.com

NON-PROFIT EXPERIENCE

City Girls Academy
Board Member, Board of Trustees (2009–Present)
Finance Chair (2009–2012)
- Led effort to consolidate financial statements and produce a comprehensive $30M budget for the entire operations

Boys and Girls Club of New York
Board Member, Board of Trustees (1992–2013)
Board Chair (2009–2010)
Finance Chair (1996–2008)
- Oversaw all of the aspects of a $20M capital project, encompassing the planning, financing, and execution of the capital campaign approved by the Board

Other
Advisory Board Member, Brooklyn Parks Trust (2010–Present)
Chair Parent Board, St. Stephens (1994–1998)
Volunteer, English as a Second Language Tutor (2008-2012)

PROFESSIONAL AFFILIATIONS

Member, American Institute of Certified Public Accountants (AICPA)
Member, Committee on Management of an Accounting Practice, Steering Committee of Financial Review, New York Society of CPAs

EDUCATION/CREDENTIALS

New York University
Bachelor of Science in Business Administration, with Concentration in Accounting

Certified Public Accountant (CPA), State of New York

Continuing Education of 40 hours annually, including tax, accounting and auditing, management and technology

OTHER INFORMATION

Fluent in Spanish ▪ Avid reader and skier ▪ Enjoy travel, cooking, and Latin dance.

Bios

Biographies, or "bios," are an alternative way of presenting your credentials. Bios streamline the information that would ordinarily be presented in a resume and present it in narrative form. Bios are used in three situations:

- For senior, experienced individuals with many notable accomplishments who wish to highlight particular themes
- For individuals, like consultants, who are providing particular types of services
- When it's more important for the potential employer or client to evaluate your competencies, networks, and major achievements rather than your career chronology

Bios are usually a few paragraphs in length, written in the third person, and fill no more than one-half to two-thirds of a page.

Like resumes, bios typically follow reverse chronological order and also include the following:

- Statement that provides an overview of your work history and significant competencies
- Description of your most recent and most noteworthy positions or accomplishments
- Brief description of previous positions held
- Mention of education and relevant personal information

You can find examples of bios on the websites of most major companies for their senior management or board members.

Any resume can be turned into a bio, and vice-versa. The following page shows an example of a bio based on the resume of Jaime Hernandez, which we saw on *pages 96–97*.

Bios

SAMPLE BIO

JAIME HERNANDEZ

Jaime Hernandez, Senior Vice President of Retail Client Services at Charles Schwab, brings over 20 years of successful management experience to his present role at the company. In his current role at Charles Schwab, Jaime oversees all client service operations. Most notably, he increased the retention of high net worth clients by over 5%, and initiated a referral program with independent asset managers, which captured $2 billion in additional assets.

Prior to assuming this role, Jaime filled other key management and financial roles throughout the company, working in the Marketing, Strategic Planning and International divisions of the company. As Vice President of the International Division, Jaime launched a business development unit targeting the growing Hispanic market in the U.S. and captured more than 5,000 accounts, representing $250 million in assets. With additional experience marketing to Asia and Europe, Jaime is considered a leading authority on marketing to ethnic and international communities.

Prior to joining Schwab, Jaime was a Strategic Planning Analyst at Grupo Alfa, a Mexican industrial conglomerate, and an instructor at Tecnológico de Monterrey, one of the top universities in Mexico.

Jaime earned a B.S. in Chemical Engineering from M.I.T. and an M.B.A. from Stanford University's Graduate School of Business.

2000 Smith Avenue • Palo Alto, CA 94111 (650) 222-5555 • jaime@yahoo.com

Marketing Plan

A marketing plan is designed to launch a product thoughtfully and effectively. In the job search or career transition process, the product is you and the competencies you have to offer. The marketing plan is a valuable tool to use in planning the next step in your career, not only during your current transition but also in years to come as you look to make each successive step in your career — whether it is an internal move in the same company or a new opportunity outside the company. A marketing plan is as beneficial to professionals working in the non-profit and government sectors as it is to those in the private sector.

WHY A MARKETING PLAN?

The act of mapping out a plan on paper makes you define more clearly what you are looking for. It requires you to articulate how you are different and what your key selling points are. Finally, writing a marketing plan focuses your efforts, helps define a thoughtful strategy, and outlines a clear path of action.

THE FOUR P'S

The four essential elements to any marketing plan are Product, Place, Price, Promotion. These apply to your marketing plan in the following ways:

PRODUCT	This is you and your competencies — the skills, knowledge, and traits that you are good at and enjoy using the most.
PLACE	Where do you want to be working? This is described by geographic area, industry, and the organization's size, culture, and structure. This also includes a list of sample target organizations.
PRICE	What are the compensation and benefits that you require? What is the package that you feel accurately represents the value you bring?
PROMOTION	How will you get the word out about your product (you!)? What networking efforts will you engage in?

OTHER ELEMENTS

Targeted position(s), a brand description (*see pages 45–48*), and your positioning statement (*see pages 53–55*) are also important elements of the marketing plan.

Your marketing plan is a living document — that is, it will change as you acquire new information and as your goals change and evolve. It is not a one-time exercise, but a tool that is constantly updated to reflect where you are in the job search or career transition process. You may have one marketing plan that reflects alternative paths, or you may draft separate marketing plans for each path.

We recommend that you show your marketing plan to others who you are asking for help in the job search or career transition process. First, it will show them that you are being extremely thoughtful about the process, which will inspire confidence in you and may lead them to offer their assistance. They can also provide good feedback and, specifically, may give helpful leads after reviewing your sample targets in terms of contacts they may have at different places, or new ideas about organizations of interest that you should explore. If you are a part-time or executive MBA student, it is also a good idea to complete an initial draft of your marketing plan prior to meeting with a counselor at your school's Career Center. It will make your session much more productive and will make it easier for the counselor to help you.

The following pages show a sample marketing plan as well as a blank template for you to use in drafting your own.

Marketing Plan

SAMPLE MARKETING PLAN

Targeted Position(s): Senior Brand Manager or Marketing Director

Brand Description: In my work I value financial gain, prestige, variety and affiliation. I am at my best in a creative business environment where I am a key contributor to a product development team. I bring my talents of understanding customer needs, communicating those needs to others, and translating those needs into products. I am known for being customer-focused and innovative. In my next role, I would like to be thought of as a strong business leader who understands the bottom line and generates results. Ten years from now, I would like to be a senior executive (possibly SVP or Partner in a consulting firm) with brand strategy responsibility for international, fashion-oriented consumer products.

Positioning Statement: I have a consumer marketing background, primarily in the cosmetics industry, where I have been involved in all stages of the product lifecycle — from market research and product development through product launch. Most recently, I was part of a team that successfully launched a new skin care line for Clinique. I want to use this experience in a brand management role for a large apparel, luxury goods, or cosmetics company like Banana Republic, LVMH, or Lancôme.

Product = Key Competencies:

Skills	Knowledge	Traits
Qualitative and Quantitative Research	Cosmetics Industry	Self Starter
Written/Verbal Communication	Prototype Creation and Testing	Collaborative
Social Media Strategy	Product Lifecycle	Detail-oriented

Place = Target Market Characteristics:

Geographic area:	New York preferred — willing to relocate for the right opportunity
Industries:	Apparel, Luxury Goods, Cosmetics
Size of organization:	Fortune 1000; international in scope
Organizational structure:	Not too hierarchical, possibly matrix organization
Culture:	Team-based, collaborative, innovative

Sample Targets:

Apparel	Luxury Goods	Cosmetics
GAP	Tiffany	Elizabeth Arden
Levi's	Sotheby's	Estée Lauder
Banana Republic	Godiva	MAC
Victoria's Secret	Hermes	Lancôme
J Crew	LVMH	Christian Dior

Price = Compensation & Benefits: $125-175K, 3 weeks vacation, training budget of $2,000

Promotion: Join Brand Marketing Association
Call boss from Clinique and ask for feedback on resume and contacts
Go to luxury goods trade show in New York
Call Jane who works for GAP
Have coffee with David from MAC Cosmetics
Apply to job postings with consumer goods companies
Ask for referrals to and meet 5 new industry contacts this month
Join LinkedIn alumni and targeted industry groups

Marketing Plan

MARKETING PLAN TEMPLATE

TARGETED POSITION(S)			
BRAND DESCRIPTION			
POSITIONING STATEMENT			
PRODUCT = KEY COMPETENCIES	Skills:	Knowledge:	Traits:
PLACE = TARGET MARKET CHARACTERISTICS	Geographic area: Industries: Size of organization: Organizational structure: Culture:		
SAMPLE TARGET ORGANIZATIONS	Industry: Targets:	Industry: Targets:	Industry: Targets:
PRICE = COMPENSATION & BENEFITS			
PROMOTION			

Marketing Plan

TARGET LIST

In addition to your summary marketing plan template, you will also want to have an expanded, more robust target list that goes beyond a few representative companies. This list should have roughly 30-50 companies on it. These should be companies that you are interested in learning more about — they don't necessarily need to be companies that you know you want to work for. You may indicate your top choices by putting them in bold font or setting them apart in some other way.

The next page shows a sample target list for an individual who is interested in the Food & Beverage industry and is open to three geographic areas — New York City, Chicago, and the San Francisco Bay Area. They have highlighted in bold the companies they are most interested in (in this example, coffee and chocolate companies). Organizing the list in the following way will make it easier for others to read and understand your goals. As with your summary marketing plan, you'll want to show your full target list to others who are in a position to help you. They may be able to identify contacts that they know at various organizations, as well as help you expand the list further by identifying organizations you didn't previously know about.

While this target list will develop over time, when approaching more senior people for help, you'll want to have a list that is quite comprehensive, as it will likely be difficult to "go to the well" several times. This list will also evolve over time as you learn more about different organizations and your target becomes more focused — some new organizations will emerge and be added to the list and others will come off the list based on other information you receive.

Marketing Plan

SAMPLE TARGET LIST

	FOOD COMPANIES	BEVERAGE COMPANIES
NEW YORK CITY	Crumbs Bake Shop Dannon Co. Inc. Magnolia Bakery Pepsico	**Green Mountain Coffee** Heineken USA SoHo Beverage Voss USA
CHICAGO	Hillshire Brands Kraft Foods Oscar Mayer Quaker Oats Company Sara Lee Corp Tootsie Roll Industries Wm. Wrigley Jr. Company **World's Finest Chocolate**	Beam Inc. **Intelligentsia Coffee & Tea** Miller Coors Pabst Brewing Company Tropicana Products
SAN FRANCISCO BAY AREA	Boudin Bakery Clif Bar Del Monte Foods Diamond Foods Dreyer's Grand Ice Cream **Ghirardelli Chocolate Company** Häagen-Dazs **TCHO** Jelly Belly La Boulange Niman Ranch Otis Spunkmeyer Planet Organics Popchips PowerBar The Republic of Tea **See's Candies**	Anchor Brewing Company **Blue Bottle Coffee** Campari America Jamba Juice Odwalla **Peet's Coffee & Tea** SKYY Spirits

Social Media

Social media has become an increasingly important resource in recruiting. According to a 2013 Jobvite survey:

- 94% of recruiters use or plan to use social media in their recruiting efforts
- LinkedIn remains the top social network, with 96% of recruiters using LinkedIn to search for candidates, 92% to vet candidates pre-interview, and 91% to post jobs
- 93% of recruiters are likely to look at a candidate's social profile and 42% have reconsidered a candidate based on content viewed in a social profile (positive and negative)

ONLINE BRAND

Given the importance of social media, it is important that your online brand be a positive one. Be mindful that your online reputation, including public photos and comments, will impact how others perceive you. Does your online presence seem professional or does it leave others with a different impression? Take a moment to search for yourself online to see what information comes up.

Although Facebook, Twitter, and other social media channels are used for recruiting, a number of professionals use LinkedIn for their professional network and Facebook for their personal contacts only.

USING LINKEDIN

Benefits

LinkedIn can be a great tool for expanding and accessing your network. Most common uses are to:

- Build connections with friends and former colleagues — types of contacts could include work colleagues, friends, alumni, or people with whom you share a common interest
- Showcase your background, skills, and experience for potential recruiters
- Research and network to get into target companies and learn more about target industries
- Find job postings as well as jobs that will be selected for you, based on your profile and preferences, as potentially interesting
- Research the background of people that will be interviewing you
- Leverage your alumni network

Guidelines

A LinkedIn profile will often be the first touch point with a new contact, whether it's a friend of a friend who looks you up before meeting you for an informational interview or a recruiter who finds your profile intriguing. In some cases, LinkedIn profiles are circulated to hiring managers before they even see a resume. As a result, it is important to take the time to create a good LinkedIn profile. Some suggestions are outlined on the following pages.

Social Media

USING LINKEDIN

General
- Always keep your profile up to date, as recruiters are increasingly using LinkedIn to source candidates who may not be actively looking for a job
- If you have a common name, consider adding a middle name or initial to avoid confusion with others
- When you are changing your profile and don't want everyone to receive activity broadcast messages of your updates, make sure you have turned off your activity feed in settings and/or change who can view your activity feed

Photo
- Yes, you need one. People connect with a picture and often will remember the face, but not always the name
- Your photo doesn't have to be professionally taken, but should be a fairly recent, professional-looking head shot. No selfies!
- Keep your brand in mind — a photo of your puppy, child, or a famous actor instead of you is not suggested!
- This is not online dating — look professional, not sexy. You want the picture to say "capable" and "successful"
- Smile

Headline
- This is what appears under your name — it may be your title or a description of what type of professional you are. For example, *"Project Leader," "Vice President of Finance"* or *"Social Media & PR Manager"*
- As always, keep keywords in mind
- If you are looking for full-time work but are currently doing consulting projects until the right opportunity comes along, you may put "Independent Consultant"

Summary
- This is a concise version of your positioning statement, or the summary from your resume
- Highlight key knowledge, skills, and traits that are most relevant for your next targeted position
- Use keywords in your summary to the extent possible to ensure you are more easily found when recruiters search LinkedIn

Experience
- There's no need to include your entire resume — just a key summary for each role is good, or highlight a few key accomplishments
- Use keywords for your targeted role, as well as skills, and competencies that you enjoy and want to continue using, to increase your chances of turning up in a recruiter's search. It's ok to be repetitive — it's all about search engine optimization

Skills & Endorsements
- Choose keywords in this section as well
- Seek endorsements. While the individual endorsements aren't important, the aggregate should showcase the skills you want to highlight going forward. If that's not the case, ask friends and colleagues to endorse you for the skills that you would like to show up higher in your list

Social Media

USING LINKEDIN

Education
- Include degrees and institutions from which they were earned

Interests
- As with your resume, you could include personal interests and subjects/industries that intrigue you

Recommendations
- Be intentional — when you complete a project or get positive feedback, ask for a recommendation on LinkedIn. It could be from your boss, a client, a peer in another department, etc. It only adds to your credibility

Other
- Include your preferred contact information so colleagues and recruiters can easily contact you

Groups
- Join relevant groups. You can make new connections and join interesting conversations about your current or desired field. In addition, the right collection of groups can help reinforce a desired brand

You can never have too many keywords in your profile. A good way to determine what words and phrases to use is to look at several job descriptions for your targeted job and to see what common words and phrases are used among them.

Working with Executive Recruiters

Executive recruiters can, at times, be a useful resource when making a career transition. The key is knowing how to work with them.

Contingent vs. retained searches

There is a difference between recruiting firms that work on a retainer basis and those that work on a contingency basis. Retained search firms are paid whether or not a hire is made for the open position. These firms tend to be the large, global executive recruiting firms like Russell Reynolds Associates, Korn Ferry, Spencer Stuart, etc. A list of some of these firms can be found in the *Useful Websites* section of the *Appendix (see page 172)*. Contingency recruiting firms are only paid if a successful hire is made. One risk to be aware of when working with contingency recruiters is the possibility they may try to sell you a job that is not right for you or is not in your best interest, so that they can earn their fee. Ask the recruiter to clarify if he is working on a retained or contingency basis.

You are NOT the client!

Executive recruiters work for the hiring company — NOT the candidate. This is a common misunderstanding on the part of job seekers. You may work with recruiters that are friendly, helpful, and encouraging — but keep in mind that they will hold the interest of the client company ahead of yours.

Executive recruiters fill specific slots

Executive recruiters will be most interested in speaking with you to the extent your profile matches a particular opportunity. In the absence of a specific, open search that you are interviewing for, forward your resume to the relevant recruiters that specialize in your industry or job function so that they have your resume — and move on! Be open to speaking with whoever is willing or available to talk to you at the executive recruiting firms, but continue with your normal job search activities. Do not sit back and wait for an executive recruiter to find you a job.

Executive recruiters look for square pegs for square holes

Executive recruiters exist to make the searches of companies simpler and more effective. They typically seek candidates with a solid track record in their industry or job function, and who have shown steady, progressive growth in responsibilities and accomplishments. These are the candidates that are most likely to be attractive to their clients and are more likely to be a successful hire. In a strong job market, executive recruiters will make more of an effort to sell your strengths, but generally speaking, executive recruiters are not looking for career changers.

Make it easy for executive recruiters to sell you to the client

Whether on your resume or in an email to the recruiter, highlight a few bullet points summarizing why you believe you are a good fit for the position you are interviewing for or seeking out. Recruiters see hundreds of resumes, so make a clear and compelling case for your candidacy.

Executive recruiters are not career counselors

If an executive recruiter is willing to meet with you (usually based on a referral), he or she may be able to give you some valuable guidance and information, such as feedback on your resume and general marketability. They can also tell you about what they've seen in the marketplace in terms of demand for certain positions, compensation ranges for recent searches they've conducted, etc. They are not paid career counselors, so don't expect them to provide endless advice about your career direction. As with any networking conversation, be respectful of the time that they offer and come with specific questions in hand.

Working with Executive Recruiters

Let the executive recruiter help you
When you are interviewing for a position sourced by an executive recruiter, ask the recruiter what the client has liked and not liked about other candidates who have interviewed for the role, what the client is looking for, what questions or concerns the client might have about your candidacy, etc. After the interview, ask the recruiter for candid feedback.

Customize communications
It's okay to email multiple recruiters at one firm with your resume, but be sure to customize the introductory email. Sending everyone an email that is obviously generic will most likely ensure that it gets thrown out.

Ask executive recruiters to spread the word
Most of the large, retained recruiting firms are quite collaborative within sectors and offices. Some recruiters might be willing to send your resume to their whole practice group with a blurb about what you are looking for. This will keep you on the radar screens of other recruiters, who may be working on searches that are a fit with your background.

Be forthcoming with compensation information
Most recruiters ask candidates for their current compensation. Unlike with internal recruiters, this is the one place where you need full disclosure, since it is standard operating procedure for executive recruiters to ask about compensation. When candidates balk or try to hold back this information, it's a red flag for executive recruiters, especially if the process is moving forward and the candidate is already meeting with the client.

Network your way in
Executive recruiting firms are no different from any other organization in that it is always better to approach a recruiter through a referral.

Actively build and maintain your network of executive recruiters
Do your best to return recruiters' phone calls — even if you are not looking for a job. Be generous, where possible, with leads and helpful information. This will make it more likely that they will respond to your calls and emails when you want to access your network of executive recruiters.

Exit Statement

Your exit statement is how you answer the question of why are you looking to leave your current job or company, or why you left your most recent job, or another specific job prior to that. There are two key guidelines when it comes to your exit statement:

1) Keep it short

With the exit statement, less is more. Don't get into long-winded details. This is especially true if you left under less-than-favorable circumstances.

2) Be positive

Don't be negative or complain about your terrible working hours, your cranky boss, or horrible commute. People don't like complainers. Take a positive spin and highlight what you enjoyed and want to have more of going forward, not what you are running away from.

Some examples include:

> "My wife and I are looking to relocate to the West Coast to be closer to family. Unfortunately, my current employer doesn't have offices there, so it requires me to look outside my current company for new opportunities."

> "What I love most about my current job is the work I do overseeing grants to youth-related programs in this region. I'd like to have a more direct impact on this community by working at a non-profit that serves inner-city youth."

> "While my current job involves a lot of numerical analysis, I've had the opportunity to do some creative work in collaboration with the marketing team. I really loved this type of creative work and am now looking to do more of it at a firm like yours, where the creative aspect is highly valued."

> "As a generalist at my consulting firm, I've gained knowledge and experience in a broad range of industries. I am now looking to focus and develop deeper expertise in the clean technology sector."

> "My company was acquired and I was part of a staff reduction that affected about 15% of employees."

> "During the last recession, the demand for my firm's services sharply dropped and a number of employees, including me, were let go."

Interview Preparation and Performance

In this section and those that follow, for convenience we refer to companies. However, all of the tools are applicable to other types of organizations as well, including non-profit, government, and entrepreneurial organizations. Once you have landed a formal job interview, prepare by taking these key steps:

STEP 1

Know the Company

Do your research by reading the company's website, searching Google for relevant news and information, and talking to people in the industry who will give you more insight into the company's:

- History
- Management and leadership
- Current performance
- Products
- Customers
- Competitors
- Culture
- Recent news coverage

STEP 2

Know the Job

Learn as much as possible about the job and the scope of responsibilities that it entails. What is the role of this position on the team? What are the activities encompassed, competencies required, and results expected? Will you be more of an apprentice learning from others, or will you be meeting with clients by yourself the first week? The same job title may mean something different at various companies, so do your best to find out in advance what it means at the company where you are interviewing.

STEP 3

Know the Interviewer(s)

Find out as much as you can about the people interviewing you. Know their roles and responsibilities in the organization and in the hiring decision. Find out what their perspectives or hot buttons are and why they care about this position. What are the problems that they hope the person in this role will solve? How will this role impact their job or department? Check LinkedIn to learn about the interviewer's background — there might be common points of connection, e.g. people in common or schools attended.

STEP 4

Know Your Competencies and Position Yourself

Make sure you have thoughtfully considered why the company should hire you.

- What are the skills, knowledge, and traits that you possess and are good at or enjoy using?
- What value can you immediately bring to the company or position?
- What problems can you solve?
- What can they rely on you to do?
- What makes you different from other candidates?

Interview Preparation and Performance

STEP 5

Have Questions Ready

The thoughtful questions you ask at the end of the interview can set you apart and show that you've done your homework. These questions also provide you with an opportunity to test your hypotheses about the company's needs and to address any concerns the interviewer may have. One thing is certain — if you are asked if you have any questions for the interviewer and your answer is no, you likely will *not* receive an offer, as it may convey a lack of interest, ambivalence, or a know-it-all attitude. Questions may naturally evolve from your conversation, and these are often some of the best questions, as they show you are engaged and curious.

Here are some additional questions you might ask a potential employer:

Company Questions:
- What are the company's top three goals?
- What are the company's strategies to acquire and keep customers?
- Where does the company hope to be in three to five years?
- How would you describe the culture?
- What competitors pose the greatest threat? Why?
- How do you see the company as being different from competitors A and B?
- What do you view as the company's greatest challenge?

People Questions:
- Why did you join this company?
- What type of people are successful here?
- What type of people don't do well here?
- What is your background?
- How would you describe the people at this company?
- What do you like best about the people you work with?

Role or Position Questions:
- In this role, what does success look like?
- What are the three most important things that the person you hire for this role needs to do really well?
- What is the contribution this role makes to the overall company goals?
- Given my background, where do you think I would contribute the most?
- What are your greatest concerns in potentially hiring me?
- If hired, what would my biggest challenge be in this role?
- What is your timing? When would you like the person for this position to be on board?
- Is there any question I should be asking that I am not asking?
- What is the typical career path within the company for someone starting in this type of position?
- If I were hired for this position, how often and in what context would you and I interact?

Interview Preparation and Performance

STEP 6 — **Practice, Practice, Practice**

Be ready for all the questions that could potentially be asked. The better prepared you are with the content of your response, the more you can pay attention to the conditions of the conversation — things like the tone of the conversation or the impact you are having on the interviewer or hiring manager. When you are confident and articulate about what you want to say, you can pay attention to building the relationship and connection with the interviewer. Most people get nervous in interviews because they put tremendous pressure on themselves to *impress* the interviewer. It is more important that you *connect* with the interviewer and build the relationship.

Practice and get feedback from peers, colleagues, or a career coach, who can also help you hone your overall presentation. We have included mock interview evaluation forms to assist in providing this feedback. These can be found on *pages 163–165* in the *Appendix*.

STEP 7 — **Maintain a Positive Mindset**

Mindset can have a huge impact on performance, whether you are an Olympic athlete or a job candidate. Going into the interview with a positive mindset like, *"I know I'm well-qualified for this job,"* or *"I'm excited to learn more about this role,"* can help you manage nerves, be more present, connect better with the interviewer, and, therefore, perform better overall. A negative mindset or attitude, such as, *"I probably won't get this job either,"* or *"I better not blow it,"* put you at a disadvantage before you even walk through the door — you are likely to interpret information with a negative bias and will be less likely to make a personal connection with your interviewer(s). The mindset we hold around anything in any given moment is a conscious choice. Before you go in to any interview, check in with yourself to see what kind of mindset you are holding about the interview, position, or yourself. If it is a negative perspective, take a step back and see if you can identify and adopt a more positive perspective — even if it is only temporary — to help you perform at your best in the interview.

Interview Preparation and Performance

COMPANY/ ORGANIZATION RESEARCH

Learning about the company or organization and the position for which you will interview is key to your preparation. Being fully prepared will allow you to feel confident in the interview and will enable you to perform at your best. Your research should include the company website, annual report (if applicable), news sources like the *New York Times* and *Wall Street Journal,* as well as conversations with current and former employees and customers. You will also want to follow a company with whom you are interviewing on LinkedIn, Twitter, and Facebook to receive real-time updates. Allow yourself approximately two hours of research, but don't go overboard. Your time is best spent practicing with mock interviews.

Use this template for your research.

CONTACT INFORMATION	**Company Name:** **Contact Name/Title:** **Phone:** **Email:**
INTERNAL FACTORS	**Management Team:** **Strengths and Weaknesses:** **Purpose/Mission and Objectives:** **Organizational Structure, Culture, and Values:** **Description of Main Products/Services:**

Interview Preparation and Performance

COMPANY/ORGANIZATION RESEARCH

PERFORMANCE

Revenues:

Profits:

Annual Growth:

Number of Employees:

Major Business/Product Lines:

_____ (_____% of revenue)

_____ (_____% of revenue)

_____ (_____% of revenue)

_____ (_____% of revenue)

IF PUBLIC

Stock Price/Market Cap:

52 Week High/Low:

P/E Ratio:

IF PRIVATE

Investors:

Funding Raised:

EXTERNAL FACTORS

Markets and Customers:

Industry Trends:

Competitors:

RECENT NEWS

Interview Preparation and Performance

TYPES OF INTERVIEW QUESTIONS

There are many kinds of interview questions. Each type of question will elicit different information from you, the candidate. Some questions are more effective than others, and you should be familiar with all of them, as hiring managers and recruiters will vary in their level of preparedness as well as in their interview skill and style.

Behavioral Questions

Behavioral interview questions are most often used, as they are highly effective and can give the interviewer telling information about your competencies. This type of question focuses on past performance — a strong predictor of future performance. Behavioral questions provide you with the opportunity to give evidence, by way of example, to the hiring manager of how, where, and when you have demonstrated key competencies that are directly associated with the job responsibilities. For example, your ability to talk about a time when you managed a crisis situation will give the interviewer confidence in your ability to do this at her company. Preparing for behavioral interviews will be discussed further in the following pages.

Examples:

- Tell me about a time when you had to resolve a conflict.
- Give me an example of a time when you influenced others.

Situational Questions

This type of question or interview structure is increasingly common. It usually involves a role-play that directly demonstrates relevant competencies to the hiring manager. This is more typical in interviews for positions in sales, customer service, and the like.

Examples:

- I am a potential client for this brokerage firm. Tell me about the company's products and enroll me as a client.
- I am an irate customer. Let's see how you handle the situation.

Pressure Questions

This type of question is less common today, but not unheard of. As the name indicates, it is meant to see how you react under pressure or in a hostile environment. Questions like this are more likely to arise in industries where the work environment may be high pressure or fast paced, such as those found in securities trading or in broadcast journalism. In posing these questions, the interviewer will likely appear abrasive or harsh. Remember, this is not about you — it is a test to see how you handle yourself and how well you retain your composure.

Examples:

- That's a ridiculous idea. What makes you think that will work?
- What makes you think we would want to hire you anyway?

Hypothetical Questions

These questions are not as effective in ascertaining your past experience, but can demonstrate your ability to be creative and think quickly. This type of question can also show how you think through a situation.

Examples:

- What would you do if a major client asked you to implement a project that was ill-conceived?
- If you were CEO of this company, what would you do differently?

Interview Preparation and Performance

TYPES OF INTERVIEW QUESTIONS

Open-Ended Questions

Open-ended questions can, at times, be directly relevant to the job responsibilities, but can also be very vague or broad. The risk in answering this type of question lies in providing too much irrelevant information. To answer these questions effectively, it is important to focus your answers and make them concise and applicable to the position.

Examples:

- What was your experience like at XYZ company?
- How would you describe your last manager?

Narrowing / Probing Questions

This approach is a series of questions where the interviewer continually narrows the focus of information and dives deeper to obtain increasingly relevant details about your experience.

Examples:

- Tell me how you value a company. Then what would you look at? In what other ways might you do this?
- Tell me about a conflict you resolved. What did you consider? How did you approach the people involved? What was the outcome? What would you have done differently?

Yes / No Questions

This type of question can be very limiting in the information it provides a hiring manager. It is your job to elaborate beyond a one-word answer to make your response as compelling as possible and relate it to the competencies required for the position.

Examples:

- Do you enjoy being on the board of the Financial Women's Association?
- Did you take any marketing electives while in business school?

Leading Questions

Leading questions suggest the desired answer through the wording and tone that are used and may put you on the defensive. These questions may also be a test to ascertain your willingness to go along with a point of view that is not necessarily your own. This presents an opportunity to respectfully disagree or present other points of view to consider.

Examples:

- Don't you think the new regulations that are being proposed will hurt our industry?
- Don't you think advertising is important in this industry?

Interview Preparation and Performance

BEHAVIORAL INTERVIEW PREPARATION

As previously mentioned, behavioral interviews are extremely common and are considered one of the most effective ways to evaluate candidates. In preparing for this type of interview, there are three key steps:

- *Step 1: Identify required competencies for the job*
- *Step 2: Prepare two to three stories that demonstrate each competency*
- *Step 3: Practice!!*

First, identify the required competencies for your targeted position (formal job descriptions will often list these), or identify the competencies that you enjoy using, if you are still exploring potential career paths or don't yet know what you want to do. Remember that competencies are a combination of skills, knowledge, and traits.

Drafting stories of when you demonstrated each competency is extremely important. Not only will these stories provide compelling evidence of your abilities, but *people remember stories*. (Note that these are not stories in the fictitious sense — they must, of course, be true!) After a long day of interviewing, an interviewer might not remember your name, but she will remember your stories if they are compelling. It is important to have a few stories prepared for each competency, as one story may reflect many competencies — and you may have already used it. Note that it is acceptable to use the same story more than once, but you do not want to overuse it!

Your stories should be both relevant and concise. They typically follow the structure of looking at a problem or situation that you encountered and any constraints that stood in your way, the actions you took, and the results that you achieved. We have laid out an example below:

Competency (Skill, Knowledge or Trait): Example — Negotiation Skills

Problem: I was negotiating a deal with a major distributor who wanted large annual revenue guarantees from our company.

Constraint: We were a young company and had little capital. This was also a major distributor that could give us access to a large customer base.

Action: I made financial models of different performance scenarios, illustrating the greater upside available to them under a "pay for performance" arrangement.

Result: We reached an agreement that gave the distributor larger upside beyond certain performance targets. We saved ourselves from making any large up-front capital investments and gained access to an important distribution channel. It was a highly profitable agreement for both parties.

Interview Preparation and Performance

Draft your stories for each competency required for your targeted position(s).

Competency (Skill, Knowledge, or Trait): _____

STORY ONE	Problem Constraint Action Result
STORY TWO	Problem Constraint Action Result
STORY THREE	Problem Constraint Action Result

Interview Preparation and Performance

Draft your stories for each competency required for your targeted position(s).

Competency (Skill, Knowledge, or Trait): _____

STORY ONE	
	Problem
	Constraint
	Action
	Result
STORY TWO	
	Problem
	Constraint
	Action
	Result
STORY THREE	
	Problem
	Constraint
	Action
	Result

Interview Preparation and Performance

Draft your stories for each competency required for your targeted position(s).

Competency (Skill, Knowledge, or Trait): _____

STORY ONE	Problem Constraint Action Result
STORY TWO	Problem Constraint Action Result
STORY THREE	Problem Constraint Action Result

Interview Preparation and Performance

Draft your stories for each competency required for your targeted position(s).

Competency (Skill, Knowledge, or Trait): _____

STORY ONE	Problem Constraint Action Result
STORY TWO	Problem Constraint Action Result
STORY THREE	Problem Constraint Action Result

©2014 Next Step Partners | www.NextStepPartners.com

Interview Preparation and Performance

These three pages list potential interview questions that you will want to prepare for.

QUESTIONS TO BE READY FOR

Personal
- Tell me about yourself.
- Take me through your resume.
- What have been the three most important events in your life?
- What is your greatest accomplishment?
- How do you define success?
- What is your greatest failure or mistake?
- How would your last manager describe you?
- Give me three words to describe yourself.
- What are your short-term and long-term career goals?
- What really motivates you?
- Tell me about a decision you have made that you later regretted.
- If you could do it all over again, what would you do differently?
- What is the most important thing on your resume? Why?
- What were you doing during this gap of time that is on your resume?
- Why did you leave your last job?
- Tell me about a difficult decision you made. How did you approach that decision and what did you consider?
- Who do you admire?
- What book have you read recently?
- Who has most shaped your life?
- What should I know about you that is not on your resume?

Management / Leadership
- What is your management philosophy?
- How do you manage people?
- Can you give me an example of a time when you motivated a team of people? What did you do?
- What are the characteristics of a good manager?
- Define leadership.
- What is your leadership style?
- Tell me about a time when you successfully resolved a conflict.
- Tell me about any leadership responsibilities that you have had.
- Give me an example of something that you have done that shows initiative.
- Give me an example of a leadership role you held where things did not go as planned.
- How do you view/react to others with strong differences of opinion?
- Someone working for you is consistently performing at a sub-par level. How do you handle this?
- How do you view/react to others with strong differences of opinion?
- Someone working for you is consistently performing at a sub-par level. How do you handle this?

Interview Preparation and Performance

QUESTIONS TO BE READY FOR

Teamwork

- How do you work within a group? What is typically the role that you play? Give me an example.
- Give me an example of a time when you successfully worked within a team.
- Can a person be a leader and a team player at the same time?
- Tell me about a time when you managed team conflict. What was the outcome?
- Tell me about a time when you were part of a team that managed a complex problem.

Job / Company / Industry

- Why are you interested in this job/company/industry?
- Tell me about an exciting new development in this industry.
- What makes you think you would be successful in this job?
- What do you think this job requires?
- Tell me about a time when your loyalty to an organization was tested.
- Given that you have no background in this field, why are you interested in it?
- Why did you spend x years as a(n) _____ and how will it help you in this job?
- What do you predict is going to happen in this industry in the next five years?
- How would you go about evaluating this business?
- What do you know about our company/industry?
- Who do you think our competitors are? Why? What do they do well that we should be concerned about?
- What other jobs are you considering?
- With what other companies are you interviewing?
- What criteria are you using to evaluate the company for which you hope to work?
- What interests you most about this position?
- What two or three things are most important to you in your job?
- What parts of the job do you think you would find the least satisfying?
- You have two minutes to describe the most relevant and specific items in your background that show you are uniquely qualified for this position.
- What would you add to our company? Why do you feel we should hire someone with your background?
- What particular expertise do you have that would lend itself well to this position?
- If you were the CEO of this company (or of your last company), what would you do differently?
- What do you think it takes to be successful in this company? In this position?
- What are the biggest short-term and long-term opportunities you see in this industry?

Interview Preparation and Performance

QUESTIONS TO BE READY FOR

Strengths / Weaknesses and Skills

- Give me an example of a time when you demonstrated creativity.
- What is your biggest weakness?
- What skills, knowledge, or traits have you most improved in the last year?
- Tell me about a time when you took on a task or project that others might have avoided.
- Describe a situation where you positively influenced the actions of others.
- Give me an example of a time when you had to complete a project with limited resources. What did you do?
- Tell me about a time when you had to make an important decision with limited information. What did you consider?
- How have you had to adapt your style to communicate with different people?
- What are some of the worst communication problems you have experienced? What do you think happened? How did you help resolve the problem and what would you do differently?
- What do you think is important in building and sustaining relationships?
- Give me an example of a time when you had to work under pressure. How did you handle it?
- Can you give me an example of your ability to sell an idea, organization, or product?
- Why should we hire you?
- How do you go about establishing credibility with a client or customer?
- We're talking to many qualified candidates. What makes you stand out from the others?
- Give me an example of one of the more complex projects you've worked on. How did you approach it? What was the outcome?
- Describe a situation where you came up with a creative solution to a problem.
- Can you give me an example of a subject you mastered in which you had no prior experience?
- Describe a situation you found difficult to manage because of competing priorities. How did you handle it?
- Where will you be able to contribute immediately?
- What do you hope to learn on the job?
- How well do you work under pressure? Give me an example.
- What was the most important lesson you learned from your prior work experience?
- How competitive are you?
- What types of people seem to rub you the wrong way?
- What has driven your success more — intelligence or hard work?
- Would you consider yourself more strategic or tactical?
- Where do you fall on the qualitative/quantitative spectrum?

Interview Preparation and Performance

PHONE/VIDEO INTERVIEWS

Phone or video conference (e.g., Skype) interviews are increasingly common, as employers attempt to manage recruiting costs. They will often screen many candidates by phone or video before determining who they will bring to the company site. With phone interviews, you cannot rely on the visual impression you would otherwise give in a face-to-face interview, nor can you read the visual cues of the interviewer — is she engaged, bored, skeptical, receptive? Hence, the quality of your voice, how well you listen, and what you actually say are that much more important. With video conference interviews, be mindful of both your appearance and surroundings.

BEFORE THE PHONE/VIDEO INTERVIEW

As a candidate, you should prepare for a phone or video interview the same way you would for an in-person interview, with a few additional steps:

Practice via phone/video

Get feedback on your voice quality (tone, pitch, pace of speech, etc.) and how it reflects your attitude, energy and enthusiasm, in addition to other qualitative aspects of your answers.

Schedule uninterrupted time

Make sure you have a place to conduct the interview that is private, comfortable, and free of loud noises and distractions (e.g., barking dogs, loud traffic).

Confirm logistics

Know who will initiate the call and at what number. Even if the recruiter or hiring manager is going to call you, make sure you have her phone number or Skype ID, just in case.

Prepare materials

One luxury of a phone or video interview is that it allows you to have relevant materials spread out in front of you. You should make sure you have:

- A copy of your resume
- A copy of the job description
- Paper and pen with which to take notes
- Notes on points you want to be sure to communicate
- Questions you have for the recruiter or hiring manager
- Your calendar (so you can schedule that in-person interview!)
- A clock or watch (to make sure you are on schedule if you have a limited amount of time)
- The company's website open, if you are in front of your computer

What if...

The interviewer is late or doesn't call when scheduled? Wait 10 minutes and then call her and say (either directly or on voicemail):

"Hi, this is _____. We had a phone/video interview scheduled at _____ a.m./p.m. today. Perhaps your meetings have run behind. I am happy to reschedule and am available today until _____, or could reschedule for another day this week if that works better. Let me know what works best for you. You can reach me at _____."

Make sure the tone of your voice is friendly and understanding, not annoyed or offended.

Interview Preparation and Performance

DURING THE PHONE/VIDEO INTERVIEW

Establish rapport

This may involve a few seconds to a few minutes of small talk to establish a connection. If you are hard-pressed to think of what to say, just ask the interviewer how her day is going so far. Get to know this person. Is she easygoing? Does she have a sense of humor? You'll need to read her tone of voice (or facial expressions, if on video) to see if she wants to chat for a few moments first or get straight to business. Let her take the lead.

Dress professionally

You do not need to wear a suit, but even if this interview is by phone, you should not be wearing your pajamas or a sweat suit. Shower and dress as though you were meeting someone for a business discussion. This will put you in a more professional and confident frame of mind. This is important for obvious reasons when talking via video conference.

Use a fixed land line

Cell phones can have problems with reception and batteries can die — or perhaps even worse, they cause that awkward split-second delay where you and the other party inadvertently speak over each other. Make sure your phone is trouble-free and make sure you speak into the mouthpiece. If you are unsure about the connection, ask if the interviewer can hear you well. With some video services — like Skype or WebEx — the sound can sometimes be distorted, so it may be better to talk by phone while viewing each other by video.

Maintain good posture

In a phone interview, the interviewer cannot see your posture — she can hear it! If you are hunched over, slouching or lying on the couch, it will show in your voice. Sitting up straight — or even walking around, is conducive to being more alert and energetic, which will contribute to your performance. In a video interview, good posture shows professionalism, attentiveness, and confidence.

Be positive

Having a positive tone when speaking is extremely helpful in engaging the interviewer and conveying your attitude, energy level, and enthusiasm — all important elements that she will consider in deciding whether to invite you back for an in-person interview.

Pay attention

Do not have any distractions near you (e.g., cell phone, food, pets) that can cause you to miss something. Be focused and alert. This will also help you to read the interviewer more effectively, when talking by phone, since you don't have the benefit of visual cues. During a video interview, as with an in-person interview, you want to maintain eye contact.

Ask for a company visit or on-site interview

At the end of the interview, the recruiter or hiring manager may extend an invitation to meet more people at the company, or she may need to first talk with others at the company and get back to you. If you think the interview went well, but it does not end with a direct invitation, state your continued interest in the position and the company and say, "*I am quite interested in this role and would be delighted to come to your offices to discuss my qualifications at greater length,*" or "*I am definitely interested in this position and am wondering if it would be possible to meet with you or your colleagues in person whenever it is convenient.*" Regardless, get clarification on next steps and timing.

Interview Preparation and Performance

INTERVIEW CHALLENGES

Even for candidates who are fairly skilled at interviewing, specific challenges may arise. These typically include:

Rambling

Rambling, or talking endlessly with no real point or direction, is an extremely common hazard. It is easy to get chatty when you are nervous. Or you may not have adequately prepared to answer a particular question and have decided to just wing it. Often, this results in a long diatribe, which loses the interviewer's attention (she will tune out), and causes you not to answer the question that was posed to you. A valuable technique to prevent yourself from rambling is to number your answers from one to three. Do not use more than three, as most people cannot keep track of more than three items at a time. Below is a sample question and three possible answers that can help you structure your response and keep you focused on the question. *Answer 1* below keeps you focused on one point; *Answer 2* allows you to discuss two main points; *Answer 3*, three topics.

QUESTION	What are the most important changes happening in our industry?
Answer 1	There are a lot of changes happening right now, but I think the *most important one* is....
Answer 2	There are *two key trends* I've seen in the industry research I've done....
Answer 3	*Three changes* really stand out in my mind. Based on the research that I have done, these changes are X, Y, and Z....

Getting stumped

Every so often you may be thrown a curveball, or may be asked a question that you are not prepared to answer. It is completely acceptable to take a moment to reflect and gather your thoughts (this is much preferred to starting to speak before you know what you are going to say!). If necessary, you can even say, *"Wow! That's a really good question. Hmm...I'd like to take the time to think about that and get back to you."* Then, be sure you actually do get back to the interviewer, either later in the conversation or in a follow-up email (tell her how you will follow up and that you will do so shortly). Your follow-through is also a potential point of differentiation in your favor.

Not understanding the question

Sometimes, it is difficult to understand the interviewer's question (not all questions are asked well, as the interviewer doesn't always know what she wants to ask!), or English may not be your first language. In this situation, before you attempt to answer the question — clarify it! It is perfectly acceptable (and recommended!) to say, *"I'm not sure I understand the question. Could you rephrase it?"* Or *"To clarify, are you asking me what I am enjoying most about the technology industry?"* You might even say, *"I'm not sure what you are trying to explore. What information would be most helpful to you?"*

Not answering the question

This can be a huge pet peeve for the interviewer. Interviewers like their questions to be answered — period. Rambling or not understanding the question can both lead to a candidate not answering the question. In your response, you may also decide to incorporate other information you would like the interviewer to know about you — which can be to your benefit, except when it is at the expense of the information that the recruiter or hiring manager was initially seeking. If you are not sure if you have answered the question and given the interviewer the information she wants, you can ask, *"Did I answer your question?"* or say, *"I just want to make sure I've answered your question before we move on...."* This will show that you are sensitive to her need to be answered, and can also demonstrate your sense of awareness or conscientiousness.

Interview Preparation and Performance

INTERVIEW CHALLENGES

Negative feelings

You may be in an interview where you have negative feelings about any number of potential subjects — your prior job, your old boss, your last bonus, the interviewer across the table from you, or your frustration with the job search. These feelings may be very real and powerful for you. You need to work through and address these emotions *outside* the interview setting and preferably *before* you start interviewing. Showing any sort of anger, resentment, or ill-will is unprofessional and an immediate turn-off to any recruiter or interviewer.

During the interview, you need to address any negatives in a *constructive way.* You may be asked to describe your last manager, who you did not like at all. Instead of saying, *"He was a dictator who micromanaged everyone on his team,"* be ready with a more tactful response like, *"I think he and I have very different management styles, but I appreciated his ability to win new business."* A natural follow-up question to be prepared for is, *"How do your management styles differ?"* This response, too, must be tactful and constructive, such as, *"He has a very directive style, whereas I prefer to collaborate with and seek input from those who work with me."*

Not having specific required experience

This can be a tough situation, especially for those who are looking to switch careers. For example, you may come from a management consulting background and want to enter a field such as venture capital or private equity, or work in the corporate development department of a company. All three of these fields/functions require transaction or deal experience, something that management consulting doesn't provide.

You never want to bluff or fake having experience you don't have. Instead, think about the specific job requirement — in this case, transaction or deal experience — and break it down into its component parts. This might include analytical skills, strategy skills, and negotiation skills. If asked the question, *"What transaction or deal experience do you have?"* your answer might sound something like, *"While working in management consulting, I did not have the opportunity to work on specific transactions or deals, given the nature of the work. However, if you look at what's involved in transactions, it's really three fundamental skill sets: analytical skills, strategy skills, and negotiation skills. Let me give you examples of where I've done all three of these...Given my track record in these three areas, I'm confident that I could perform well in a deal-centric business."*

Likewise, you may be switching industries and may not yet be as well-versed as some other candidates coming directly from that industry. When asked a question like, *"Why should we hire you when we can hire someone directly from this industry?"* your answer might be something like, *"As mentioned earlier, my background in consulting has given me a lot of comfort dealing with senior executives and I've been able to demonstrate my resourcefulness in multiple client projects — two things that I know are very important for this job. As a consultant, I've also had to get up to speed quickly on new industries to achieve 'expert status' in just a few weeks to be able to serve my clients, who have often been in their industries for 20–30 years or more. Given this, I'm confident that I could get up to speed just as quickly in this industry as well."* Giving good examples of where you've learned quickly in the past and expressing your confidence in your ability to do so can be compelling to the interviewer, and can put concerns in this area to rest.

Interview Preparation and Performance

INTERVIEW CHALLENGES

Failure/weakness questions

Failure and weakness questions are essentially self-awareness questions. The interviewer wants to see if you can (1) make an honest assessment of yourself, (2) demonstrate how you have learned and grown from the failure or improvement feedback you've received, and (3) describe how your behavior has changed since then. With either of these questions, there is also the opportunity to show authenticity. It is a delicate balance — you don't want to give examples that either represent false modesty (e.g., *"I work too hard"*) or scare the interviewer away (e.g., *"I'm not great with numbers"* when interviewing for an analytical job).

With the failure question, you may also give an example that incorporates your personal life. For example, your answer might be something like, *"My biggest failure was during the time when I was working in New York. I really neglected my personal relationships and my prior professional contacts. I was so focused on my job and what was right in front of me, that when I lost my job during the last economic downturn, my support system wasn't there. It was my own fault, since I hadn't done a good job of nurturing my relationships. It was a painful lesson. I now make a conscious effort to stay connected to friends and former colleagues — even if I don't get to see them very often. It's amazing what an email or quick phone call can do to stay connected with others."*

The weakness question may be asked alone, such as *"What is your greatest weakness?"* or it may be asked as *"What is your greatest strength and your greatest weakness?"* Regardless of which way it is asked, you'll want to share what you consider to be your greatest strength (or one of them), as our weaknesses are typically the flip side of our strengths. Your answer to either question might sound something like, *"I believe our weaknesses are the flip side of our strengths, so let me start with the latter. One of my strengths is that I am an incredibly loyal person — to my friends, colleagues, family, etc. The flip side of this strength is that I can have a hard time saying 'no' when I need to. I've been getting better at this over the last few years and have been practicing setting boundaries and saying 'no' when I need to."* You will want to have at least two such strength/weakness pairings to be safe, as you might be asked for more than one.

Salary Questions

Salary questions can come up in the very first meeting. This often catches candidates off guard. Two questions are frequently asked: (1) *"How much did you make in your previous job?"* or (2) *"What are you looking to make in your next job?"* Either way, your goal is to *take the question off the table* when talking to an internal recruiter or hiring manager. The one exception where you do need to disclose your compensation is when working with an executive recruiter (*see pages 113–114* for *Working with Executive Recruiters*). However, when working with an internal recruiter or hiring manager, you don't want to discuss compensation until you are at an offer stage, when your negotiating power is the greatest (*see pages 149–157* on *Negotiation*). Right now, you still need to convince the interviewer that you are the right person for the job.

One way of tactfully taking the salary question off the table, regardless of which question above is asked, is to say:

- *"I understand compensation is an important issue and one of several factors to consider. At this point, I'm not concerned about us being able to reach an agreement on this, so I would prefer to address this when we are at an offer stage."*

What is good about this response is that it not only acknowledges merit to the question, but it also expresses your optimism and good faith that you are two reasonable parties who can come to an agreement when the time is appropriate. It helps to build trust.

Interview Preparation and Performance

INTERVIEW CHALLENGES

Salary Questions

If asked specifically about your prior compensation (which, unless you are doing the same job as before, is not relevant!), other potential responses are:

- *"I am coming from an industry with a significantly different pay scale, so any comparison would not be very meaningful."*
- *"My responsibilities in my prior role were more junior to this position, so I don't think it provides a good benchmark."*
- *"Unfortunately, my former employer experienced a major downturn in its business, so salaries were frozen for the past three years and bonuses were negligible. Thus, my prior compensation doesn't adequately reflect where I should be today."*

If asked what compensation level you are looking for in your next job, you might say any (or all) of the following responses:

- *"I don't feel that I know enough about the position yet to give you an accurate figure, so I would prefer to discuss this when I have more information about the role."*
- *"I'm still doing my due diligence on compensation ranges for this type of role. I don't feel like I have enough data to give an informed answer at this point."*
- *"I would actually look to you to indicate what range you are budgeting for this position."*

It is important to be calm and natural when responding to the salary questions — you do not want to seem defensive, secretive, or evasive, as you will risk deteriorating the trust you are trying to build with the employer. If your back is against the wall, and you are forced to disclose a number after using the above responses, always provide a range from a number that you consider to be fair and reasonable (or market value) to your ideal number that you would be thrilled to get. You should also frame your response in terms of total compensation (not just base salary) and can also frame your answer based on next year's expected compensation. For example, you might say something like, *"If I were to stay at my current company, my compensation at the end of the year would go up to X for the following year."* This will anchor the employer to a higher number. It also represents the opportunity cost of leaving your current organization (even if that is what you want to do!).

Prior to any interview, do your homework to find out compensation levels in the industry or function, or at that specific company, so you can be best prepared. More is said on this in the *Negotiation* section.

Interview Preparation and Performance

CLOSING THE INTERVIEW

Closing the interview is an important part of the process. Many people fail to do this properly, if at all. Closing an interview well can help you to build forward momentum, as well as ease some of your anxiety and uncertainty after the interview. In essence, you are aiming to close the sale.

To properly close the interview, you should:

Thank the interviewer

Let the interviewer know that you sincerely appreciate the time she has spent with you, given how busy she is, and that it was a pleasure to meet her.

Reiterate your interest

Let the interviewer know that your discussion has only reinforced your interest in the role, and that you are excited about the prospect of working together or at the company.

Ask if the interviewer has any outstanding concerns about your qualifications

Many people feel awkward asking this — but it does not have to be awkward. When done well, asking this question shows a high level of maturity and desire to discuss openly where you stand as a candidate. Many interviewers, either because of their lack of skill in interviewing, or awkward feelings, will not voice actual concerns unless asked, such as *"I don't know if he is assertive enough for this sales position."* Or, *"She's smart and articulate, but I'm not sure about her quantitative skills."* Without putting the interviewer on the spot, you can easily ask something like, *"I know we only have a few minutes left, so I just wanted to check in to see if you have any concerns or hesitations about my candidacy, so that we could discuss these areas while I'm here."* If you feel that you have "nailed" the interview and the interviewer has expressed clear interest in bringing you back for more interviews, you may not feel the need to ask this question.

Ask about next steps and timing in the hiring process

It is good to know what the hiring process is at the company. How and when will the final decision be made and who will be involved in making it? Are they having a meeting internally to discuss who will be called back or given an offer? Do they still have to interview three other candidates? Is the next step a meeting with the department head, Human Resources, or a full day consisting of six to eight interviews? Also, you should ask by when the company hopes to call people back or extend offers. If the response is "within two weeks" and you haven't heard anything for a day or two, you will know there is no need to stress.

Ask when it would be okay for you to follow up

If the interviewer indicates that she will be contacting you in one week, ask her if it would be okay for you to contact her if you haven't heard from her in two weeks. You can say, *"I understand that sometimes things run behind due to other work commitments. If I haven't heard anything in two weeks, would it be okay for me to contact you?"*

Make sure you get the interviewer's business card

If the interviewer hasn't already given you her card, make sure you ask for it so that you can follow up with a thank-you note. If she doesn't have a card with her (or ran out), make sure to write down her first and last name and get her email address. Otherwise it will be easy to forget, and it is not unheard of to be quizzed by subsequent interviewers at the company about who you've spoken to previously.

Interview Preparation and Performance

THANK-YOU NOTES

Thank-you notes are a common courtesy and should always be sent, regardless of how well or poorly you think you performed. Thank-you notes should be brief, somewhat customized by referencing your conversation, and *sent promptly!*

If decisions are being made very quickly, send your thank-you note by email that day. If the process allows you more time, and your handwriting is reasonably legible, a handwritten note on professional quality stationary can be a nice touch that makes you stand out from others. Note that handwritten letters should still be mailed within 24 hours of the interview.

Below is an example of a thank-you note sent by email:

> To: Robert Krauss
> From: Michelle Townsend
> Subject: Thank You
>
> Robert,
>
> Thank you for taking the time to meet with me today to discuss my qualifications for the Director of Operations position at Home Depot. I enjoyed hearing about your background as a construction manager and how that led to your career with the company. I also was delighted to hear about the visibility into different parts of the organization that the operations role would provide and the ease of lateral mobility within the company.
>
> Our meeting only reinforced my interest in the position, and I am confident that my operations experience in the retail sector and my passion for home improvement will allow me to make a strong contribution to the company.
>
> Thank you again for your time and consideration, and I look forward to the prospect of being part of the Home Depot team!
>
> Best regards,
>
> Michelle Townsend

Job Search Productivity

While you search for a job, you are essentially operating your own company, or single-handedly managing a product launch — you! As with any operation, improving your productivity pays off in more opportunities and a greater return on the effort invested. In your job search, when are you the most productive? What could you do more of (or less of) that would increase your productivity? What obstacles stand in the way of your being productive? What are some approaches to removing these obstacles?

Fill in the boxes below and brainstorm with some friends, colleagues, or a coach to help improve your productivity.

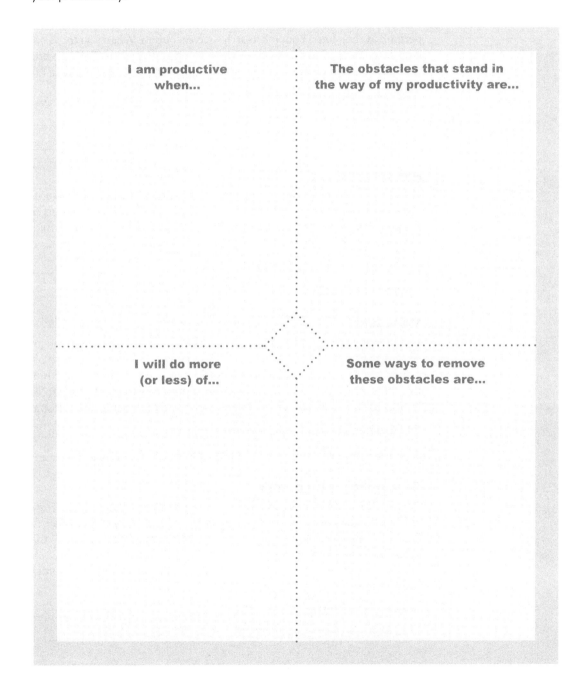

Getting Unstuck

It is normal to feel stuck during the career transition or job search process. Feeling stuck is a normal part of change. If change were easy, we would have already done it. Feeling stuck can happen at various stages of your career transition: introspection, exploration, or the job-search execution phase.

There are various strategies you can employ to get unstuck. Jot down your answers to the prompts after each question:

STRATEGIES TO EMPLOY

Take a break
Soldiering through isn't always the best strategy. Try taking a break — it can open you up to new ideas. Studies have shown that rest periods are crucial in helping both athletes and corporate executives perform at their best. Your job search is no exception. When you focus on the same problem for too long, it can be hard to come up with new or innovative ideas. Taking a break will help energize you and may also provide the fresh perspectives that will help you to move forward.

A way I can take a break this week is: _____

The benefit for me of taking a break is: _____

_____

Ask for help
The job search can be lonely. Connecting with others — whether they are friends, family, former colleagues, or a coach — can make you feel supported and understood and can help jump start the process by offering new ideas, actions, and possibilities. Brainstorming together can result in a renewed sense of hope and energy and can reinvigorate your search.

Someone I know who will be supportive is: _____

Someone who might provide new perspectives and ideas is: _____

Volunteer
Volunteering is a great way to keep your skills fresh and your confidence up. When you volunteer, you discover that even when you are feeling down, you have things to offer of value. Volunteering can also remind you that your own setbacks may be relatively minor compared to those experienced by others. Finally, volunteering can be an opportunity to meet new people who may be in a position to help you (including other volunteers and board members), and can spark new ideas.

An organization I could explore volunteering with is: _____

A person I know who might benefit from and welcome my help is: _____

Circle back with people
People often think of networking as a "one and done" phenomenon. They have an initial meeting and figure if there was any benefit, it would have occurred already. This is limited thinking. Consider your initial meetings with people to be relationship-building in nature — the first step in a long-term process. Circling back to people you initially spoke with a few months ago is also a good way to get unstuck. They may have new information and you may have new information, as well, since you last spoke.

A strong tie I could reconnect with is: _____

A weak tie I could reconnect with is: _____

Getting Unstuck

NEXT STEP PARTNERS

STRATEGIES TO EMPLOY

Picture the marathon

A career transition can be a marathon. It's exhausting, may take longer than you initially planned, and at the same time has a beginning and an end. An athlete running a marathon acknowledges how he or she is feeling at a particular point, but instead of using that to judge the whole event, thinks about his or her strategy going forward and what will get them to the finish line.

If this were a marathon, what mile mark are you on now? _____

How does that athlete feel? _____

What's your best strategy for making it to the finish line? _____

_____

_____

Managing Job References

Once an organization decides that it is interested in engaging you, the hiring manager will typically ask for references. This may be done before a formal offer is extended, to determine if an offer will actually be given, or after a formal offer is extended, in which case the offer is usually contingent upon the reference check yielding favorable information.

Because providing references from a past employer is an important element in the job search, it is important to maintain good relationships with *at least* one person (preferably your direct manager) at each of your prior employers. Plant the seed in advance — when leaving a position, or finishing a client project, ask your colleagues if you can call upon them as references in the future.

When providing references, keep the following points in mind:

Request permission first to use someone as a reference

It is common courtesy to ask a former colleague or client if he or she would be willing to serve as a reference before giving his or her name and contact information to a potential employer. A reference check should never be a surprise.

Provide at least one reference per prior employer for the last few jobs

Providing this breadth shows that you have done a good job of keeping in touch with people and have built strong relationships. It also helps you to establish a track record of credibility and can help you to build a positive reputation when a number of people from various prior employers all say good things about you.

Provide a 360° perspective

When selecting references, don't limit yourself to your direct manager (particularly where you didn't actually see eye-to-eye with your boss). Consider offering references who worked with you as peers and direct subordinates — or even your manager's boss. Their perspectives are often helpful as well. Also consider parties external to your prior employers, such as clients with whom you worked closely.

Give your references a "heads up"

Let your references know when someone might be calling them. Provide the name of the person and company that your references should expect the call from, so that they can be sure to return the call.

Coach your references

This is not a time to be modest. By this stage in the process, you should have a clear sense as to what competencies are important to succeed in the position. Let your references know what areas would be most helpful for them to talk about, and remind them of projects or work you did that you believe best reflects these desired competencies.

For example, *"I appreciate your willingness to serve as a reference. It would be most helpful if you could speak to my ability to work in ambiguous environments with little direction, as that is a key element to this job. I think the marketing strategy project I worked on last year is a good example of this."* You may consider asking each of your references to emphasize complementary competencies, as well as similar competencies. For example, you may ask one reference to speak to your client skills, and another to speak to your ability to work under pressure, while asking all of your references to speak to your presentation skills so that specific message is sure to get across.

Managing Job References

Create a reference sheet

Create a one-page reference sheet that lists each reference, his or her title and company name (indicating the company where you worked together, if he or she is no longer there), your relationship to this person at work, and the relevant contact information. A sample reference sheet follows:

RACHEL LEVIN

1800 Pacific Avenue (415) 555-3333
San Francisco, CA 94123 rachel@gmail.com

References

Bob Smyth
Vice President, Customer Service
Oracle
bob.smyth@oracle.com
(650) 555-1111
Direct manager

Susan Varlanges
Vice President, Customer Service
Salesforce.com
susan.varlanges@salesforce.com
(415) 555-4444
Direct manager

Kylie O'Connor
Manager, Customer Service
SAP
kylie.oconnor@sap.com
(650) 555-2222
Peer with whom I served on a cross-functional task force

Sanjay Patel
CFO
American Foods
spatel@americanfoods.com
(323) 555-1234
Client whose account I served for three years while at SAP

Trevor Taylor
Associate Account Representative
SAP
trevor.taylor@sap.com
(650) 555-4321
Direct report

Managing Timing of Offers

If you are fortunate to be progressing in your interviews with multiple organizations that look likely to move to an offer stage, an important question often arises – How do you influence the timing of these offers, such that you can have the opportunity to assess and compare each offer relative to the others to make the best choice possible (not to mention being able to use other offers as negotiation leverage)?

When employers extend an offer, they typically want to close on the offer quickly. If you are still in the interview process with other organizations, you will need to do two things:

1) Ask the organization that extended the offer for more time

While the offering company may be eager to get things wrapped up, don't be pressured. Some companies will issue what they call an "exploding offer," meaning that it is valid until a specified date. These dates can, and have been, extended. In the rare cases when they are not extended, you need to ask yourself if you want to work for an organization that would put you in that position or would be that inflexible. Whether or not the offer has a deadline, you can ask for more time. Two weeks is a fairly reasonable time to take to consider an offer and try to wrap up other discussions.

Spouses are also good excuses to buy more time, since you will want to discuss the offer/opportunity with them. If there is a relocation involved, you can also buy more time by asking the company to pay for a visit of the local area with your spouse so he/she can assess if this is a move that they want to make as well. These trips can take time to set up and can allow you to extend the window for you to advance your conversations with other potential employers.

Below are sample scripts that can be used to request more time.

> *"I will need some time to discuss this with my spouse as this will affect her and our family as well. I will get back to you once we've been able to go through everything. If moving to Phoenix is something she is, in fact, willing to consider, she'll also want to plan a visit first to see what it might be like to live there, as well as check out the local real estate market and schools for our kids, before we formally accept the offer."*

> *"I am really excited by this opportunity. I am approaching the offer stage with another company (or a few other companies!) and would like some time to see those conversations through. I hope you can appreciate that I'd like to make a fully informed decision, to the extent possible, as this is an important step in my career. So I'd appreciate another week or two to get back to you."*

When you do get back to them, it will not necessarily be to accept the offer (if that is where you are leaning), but to schedule the negotiation call, which can buy you some more time as well.

2) Ask the other potential employer(s) if they can expedite their process

On the flip side, you then need to get other companies to move more quickly, which can be a challenge due to their travel schedules and other pressing business they may have. To do this, you may say something like:

> *"I am approaching the offer stage with another company, and your company is one of my top choices, so I'd love to be able to consider an offer from you, if you are inclined to move in that direction. Would you be able to expedite the interview process?"*

Sometimes they will be able to accommodate you and you can align the timing of the offers — and sometimes you may have to make a decision with imperfect information.

Managing Timing of Offers

OTHER CONSIDERATIONS

A few final notes — a company from whom you received an offer may ask you what specific company(ies) you either received an offer from or are still interviewing with. You are under no obligation to share that information! You might say something like, *"I'm talking with other key players in this industry,"* or *"I'm talking to a variety of organizations, some of which are in this industry and some aren't"* — *"My offer is from a reputable technology company."* The goal is not necessarily to be evasive for it's own sake but to maintain some mystery (or privacy!) to get the company to put its best foot forward in its offer to you.

Another tactic recruiters have sometimes used is to say, *"Oh, once you get your offer, let us know what it is and we'll put together our offer for you."* Do not do this! Basically, if you tell them that Company A is going to pay you $100,000, then they will offer $100,001. You want to first see what offer they come up with, independent of your other offer(s), as it could be much higher and you will have a good understanding of how they value you. You can respond by saying, *"The other company has asked me to keep the terms of my offer confidential. I look forward to hearing the offer you put together and I can then let you know how it compares."* Or, you may just say, *"It was a fairly competitive offer. I look forward to hearing the package you put together."* You may also then have a pre-offer discussion to give them some general guidance as to the elements of an offer that are most important to you, as referenced on *page 153*.

Evaluating Job Offers

At many times in our careers, a new opportunity — even multiple opportunities — may arise. To help you decide what path or opportunity is the best involves more than weighing the pros and cons.

Title, compensation, vacation time, etc., are each important elements in evaluating an opportunity, but they are only part of what creates satisfaction and success. Integral to achieving a greater sense of fulfillment, success, and effectiveness are an environment and a job that are consistent both with our values (what we deeply believe is important) and with our vision (where we see ourselves going). Finally, evaluating job offers based on our values and vision is also an effective way to remove some of the outside influences or "shoulds" (*see page 22*) that might otherwise lead to inauthentic career choices.

VALUES

The values matrix below can help you assess which opportunity is best for you. Refer back to the values list that you developed on page 26. Transfer this list to the table below. You may rank these values in relative importance to each other by allocating 100 percentage points among them. Then, rate on a scale of 0 to 10 how well each job rates on each value, with 0 meaning "This job does not at all allow me to express this value," and with 10 meaning "This job allows me to fully express this value." You may either add up absolute point values or come up with a weighted average by multiplying the percentage weighting by the rating for each value.

Values Table

VALUE	WEIGHT	JOB 1		JOB 2		JOB 3	
	Percent x	Rating (0–10)	= Score	Rating (0–10)	= Score	Rating (0–10)	= Score
Example: Autonomy	30%	9	2.7	5	1.5	7	2.1
1.							
2.							
3.							
4.							
5.							
6.							
7.							
8.							
9.							
10.							
TOTAL SCORE	100%						

Evaluating Job Offers

VISION — Opportunities may also be evaluated by how consistent they are with your short- and long-term vision. Refer back to your notes for your five-year vision on *pages 31–34*. Identify the various attributes of your vision and list these in the table below. You may weight each attribute of your vision and score each job similarly to the values table on the previous page. Rate each job opportunity on a scale of 0–10, with 0 meaning *"This job is not at all consistent with my vision,"* and 10 meaning *"This job is completely consistent with my vision."*

Note that a job may be very consistent with your values but not with your vision, and vice versa.

Vision Table

ATTRIBUTE OF PROFESSIONAL VISION	WEIGHT Percent x	JOB 1 Rating (0–10)	= Score	JOB 2 Rating (0–10)	= Score	JOB 3 Rating (0–10)	= Score
Example: International Scope	10%	3	.3	8	.8	7	.7
1.							
2.							
3.							
4.							
5.							
6.							
7.							
8.							
9.							
10.							
TOTAL SCORE	100%						

Evaluating Job Offers

OTHER FACTORS TO CONSIDER

Option value

When considering alternative opportunities, it is important to consider the job's option value — that is, what doors does accepting a particular job close and what doors does it leave open or even create? Consider not only your next career step but also the step beyond it.

Brand value

What is the brand equity of each organization you are considering? Is it a leader in its industry that is known worldwide, or is it a regional firm or even a small non-profit or start-up that has yet to build its brand? While the brand value of the organization should not be the sole factor influencing your decision, it is an important factor in looking at your long-term career development. Since many people change jobs early in their careers, having a strong brand name on your resume can carry you further when you are looking to make a change. Working at well-known organizations like The Clinton Foundation, Microsoft, Google, Amazon, Bain, or Goldman Sachs are indicators of passing selective screening processes and will often give you more flexibility later in your career to participate in riskier, less proven ventures. However, it is not always easy to go from a smaller, lesser known company to a large industry leader. Please note that we are not advocating that you always choose well-known organizations for this reason. You may decide that you have sufficient brand names on your resume already, or are better suited to a smaller organization with a less recognizable name — in which case, you may still capitalize on the brands of your customers and clients!

Negotiation

Negotiating your own compensation and benefits can be anxiety-provoking and often causes great stress among job-seekers. Negotiation is a learned skill that you can improve upon over time with practice and experience. Being prepared with a sound strategy can greatly improve your effectiveness.

STEP 1 — Do your homework

Ask industry and company insiders and do research online (ideally, *before* you start interviewing) what the typical compensation range and structure are for the type of position you are seeking, given your experience level and market conditions. Having a range of data points will assist you in your negotiation. Knowledge is power! Some questions you may ask include:

- What is the compensation range for people at this level in the industry/at this company?
- Given my past experience, what compensation range do you feel would be appropriate?
- What compensation range would you consider to be fair for this job? What would you consider to be generous?
- What is the approximate split between base salary and bonus for this job?
- What is a typical stock option package at this level?

Where possible, you want to speak in generalities (i.e., "what does *one* typically make?" as opposed to "what do *you* make?") and refer to ranges. Specific data points are always helpful (for example, finding out that a friend of yours received an offer at one of your target companies for $125,000 with a 10% bonus is useful), and knowing what range of offers have been given is even more helpful.

In informational interviews, you might ask, "*In exploring this particular career path, I'm also doing some due diligence on typical compensation ranges for this type of role, so I can be fully prepared should I receive an offer from one of my target companies. Any information you can provide here — whether it's an overall range or specific data points you may be aware of — would be helpful. I'm happy to share with you a summary of the information I collect.*" This last part is extra incentive for the person you are speaking with to be helpful.

If you are a part-time or executive MBA student, or an MBA alumna(e), the Career Center at your business school is also a good resource for salary data and trends.

STEP 2 — Know where you stand

Identify the following three compensation figures (either in terms of base salary or total compensation):

a) Ideal: _____

b) Fair and Reasonable: _____

c) Rock Bottom: _____

The "ideal" is a number that you would be ecstatic with; the "fair and reasonable" number reflects the market rate that you would be content with; the "rock bottom" number is the minimum compensation number, beneath which you either couldn't financially support yourself or you would just not feel valued. As part of this exercise, know your walk-away point. What is your next best alternative worth? This option may simply be more time to find a better opportunity.

Negotiation

STEP 3 **Know what benefits you care about most**

In addition to base salary, identify what cash and noncash benefits or perks are of the greatest value to you.

Examples:	Ranking	Describe
Equity compensation*	_____	_____
Vacation	_____	_____
Unpaid time off	_____	_____
Comp time	_____	_____
Title	_____	_____
Training budget	_____	_____
Telecommuting	_____	_____
Flexible schedule	_____	_____
Administrative support	_____	_____
Mid-year review	_____	_____
Performance targets/bonuses	_____	_____
Signing bonus*	_____	_____
Retention bonus	_____	_____
Relocation*	_____	_____
Parking	_____	_____
Delayed start date	_____	_____
Geographic mobility	_____	_____
Ability to attend key conferences	_____	_____
Severance*	_____	_____
Other	_____	_____

* A few of the above negotiable elements warrant additional comments below.

EQUITY COMPENSATION

Equity compensation is a popular component of compensation packages, for both public and private companies, with the latter category mostly comprised of start-ups. While you want to get as much compensation in your base salary as possible, since bonuses and raises are often calculated as percentages of your base salary, equity can be an important component of compensation and is another negotiable aspect of your job offer.

Some companies will offer stock grants (actual shares of stock) and others will offer stock options (an option to buy shares of stock at a specific price, known as the strike price). There are also two types of stock options, nonqualified stock options and incentive stock options. These three different types of equity compensation (stock grants, nonqualified stock options, and incentive stock options) have different tax treatments. We recommend you consult with a tax advisor to fully understand the tax implications of the equity component of your compensation. Further, you'll want to know what the vesting schedule is for the equity. Annual vesting over three to four years is typical. Some senior executives can negotiate to receive accelerated vesting of their equity in the event of a change in control (e.g., if the company gets acquired or goes public).

Negotiation

SIGNING BONUSES

Employers typically have the most flexibility in offering signing bonuses, since it is a one-time expense for them. A signing bonus may be part of an initial offer, or it may be added (or increased) to sweeten the deal. As with a moving allowance (*see the following page*), you can ask for your signing bonus to be net of taxes, as the bonus will be taxed, leaving you with less. For example, if they offer you a $15,000 signing bonus, you can ask that the $15,000 be *net* of taxes. As with anything that they offer, or add to your compensation package, you should always express your appreciation before asking for more! You might phrase the request as, *"I very much appreciate the signing bonus (or the increase of the signing bonus). What would make it even more meaningful, is if the amount you offered is provided after tax."*

Other considerations that will be in your favor in requesting either a signing bonus, or a larger signing bonus than originally offered, are:

Missed year-end bonus or equity awards

If you are being offered a position that would require you to leave your job mid-year or later, where you normally would have received a sizable year-end bonus, a signing bonus can compensate for this loss. The same goes for equity at your current employer that would otherwise have vested if you stayed until year-end. You might say, *"If I were to accept this job, I'd be missing out on my year-end bonus in just a few months, estimated to be $50,000 this year. What can you offer to help make me whole on this front?"*

Large capital expenditure required on your part

Your new job may require that you commute to an area not served by public transportation, requiring you to buy a car if you don't already own one. This is a large capital expense on your part and a company will often be willing to contribute to this additional cost in the form of a signing bonus (or an increased signing bonus). Here you might say, *"I'm really excited about this opportunity. It would require that I buy a car to commute to your offices, which I'm happy to do, but it is a large cash outlay for me. I've researched compact cars with good mileage, and the average starting price is about $30,000. What can you offer to help offset this expense that I would need to incur?"*

Negotiation

RELOCATION

There are several aspects of relocation and different ways that your relocation package can be handled.

Common elements of relocation packages include:

- Trips to the new location in advance of the move to search for housing
- Physical moving of belongings, family members, pets, and cars
- Temporary housing in the new location until permanent housing is found
- Storage of belongings until a new home is found
- Broker's fees to sell your current home, if owned
- Closing costs on your new home, if purchased
- Broker's fees to find your new home, if renting
- Stipend to make repairs and improvements necessary to sell your current home
- Trips home to manage the sale of your home if it is not sold prior to the move
- Additional compensation to make up your initial investment, if forced to sell your home at a loss
- Additional compensation to help pay for taxes, if your home is sold at a profit
- Career transition support for your spouse, if he/she is forced to leave his/her job due to the relocation

When it comes to the physical move, employers may use any of the following approaches:

Self-move with reimbursement of expenses up to a specified level

The advantage of this approach is that you can choose your own mover and handle things the way you'd like, and are reimbursed up to a certain level. The downside is mostly the administrative hassle and cash outlay for expenses. It is up to you to manage and arrange for everything. You also need to keep a detailed log of receipts and will need to spend the money upfront and may have to wait several weeks or longer for reimbursement.

Lump-sum fixed stipend to cover moving costs

With this approach, the incentive is for you to keep costs low, as you will be able to pocket the balance of the stipend (assuming it is large enough to begin with to cover everything). You will also typically need to arrange for everything and manage it yourself, including handling payments to the mover. Since you will receive a lump-sum check, it will be viewed as compensation and therefore will be taxed, effectively leaving you with a lot less than the gross amount. This is a good reason to ask for the stipend offered to be grossed-up for taxes in your negotiations. For example, if you are offered a relocation stipend of $10,000, you should ask to receive $10,000 after taxes, so the gross amount given to you would be higher.

Moving expenses paid directly by the employer

This tends to be the easiest and the most hassle-free approach. The employer has an approved vendor it works with and is typically billed directly, so you don't have to worry about any cash outlays or any administrative hassle.

SEVERANCE

When negotiating an offer with an organization that has a decent amount of risk involved, it is possible to negotiate severance upfront, should things not work out. This is more common for more senior professionals, but is not out of the question for others, when someone is being lured away from a very stable job for a new, less certain opportunity. The terms are usually such that if the individual is terminated without cause — where cause is specifically defined as gross negligence or criminal misconduct — a certain amount of severance pay and, potentially, career transition support will be provided.

Negotiation

STRATEGIES TO EMPLOY

There are many strategies to employ when negotiating your compensation and benefits. You may find that using a combination of the strategies below is most helpful.

Have a pre-offer discussion

The hiring manager or HR representative may indicate that the company wants to move to the offer stage. You now have the opportunity to let the other party know what elements of the package are most important to you or to give other guidance. You might say, *"That's wonderful! I am looking forward to seeing the package that you will put together. It may be helpful for you to know what is most important to me in considering this offer is having most of my compensation in base salary versus bonus, as well as ample vacation time and a relocation package."* The idea here is to give broad guidance while not dictating specific terms, so the starting point for the negotiation is more advanced.

Set the tone

In any negotiation discussion, you always want to set the proper tone that indicates that you are (1) excited by the opportunity or prospect of working at the company, and (2) that you are a reasonable person who is negotiating in good faith. A good opening phrase is, *"I am really excited about this offer. I have a few questions, which I'm sure we can talk through to come to a resolution that works for both of us."* In saying this, you are putting yourself on the same side as the hiring manager, with both of you working together toward the same goal — rather than making yourself an adversary in a zero-sum game.

Always negotiate

Know that your negotiating power is the greatest once you have received the offer — **so use it!** Many people, either out of timidity, inexperience, or dire need for closure, do not negotiate their offers and leave money on the table unnecessarily. Many recruiters or hiring managers do not put forth their best offer initially. Many elements (whether cash or noncash in nature) may be negotiated for. There are some jobs in fact — such as in business development or venture capital — where they *expect* you to negotiate because it is a core skill required for these positions.

Do not respond immediately

When an offer is communicated to you, listen and take in the information. You may express excitement about the company's decision to offer you employment, but simply say, *"I am so excited to have gotten an offer! Let me take some time to digest the information you've given me and I'll get back to you in the next few days with any follow-up questions."* If they ask what you think of the offer, hold your cards close to you vest and say as little as possible, other than expressing excitement about having received an offer. You want to avoid comments like, *"This is fantastic!"* or *"It's much higher that I thought it would be,"* that would only serve to reduce your ability to negotiate more. If anything, you can say something like, *"It seems like a credible offer* (if, in fact, you think it is), *but I would like some more time to digest it."* Hiring managers typically want to move quickly, so 48 hours is usually the standard time frame in which to get back to them for a follow-up discussion (not necessarily with your answer!).

Talk to the decision maker

Usually this is the hiring manager. While Human Resources is sometimes involved in the process, they are usually not the decision maker. HR may initially communicate the offer to you or process the written offer letter, but your follow-up discussion should be with the hiring manager. You can let HR know this by saying, *"Thank you for this information. I am going to review it and will follow up directly with Dave [the hiring manager] with my questions since, as my manager, he'd be best able to answer my questions."*

Negotiation

STRATEGIES TO EMPLOY

Don't take it personally

For many people, particularly those with a preference for harmony and an aversion to conflict or confrontation, negotiating can be particularly challenging or stressful. Recognize that this is not about *you* as a person. Nor is it about being *liked*. The hiring manager will continue to think highly of you as long as you conduct yourself ethically and professionally. Try to seek some emotional distance to improve your effectiveness as a negotiator. If necessary, pretend you are negotiating on behalf of "a client."

Start with base salary

When prioritizing what to negotiate for, always start with the biggest item, which is typically base salary. If you are going to negotiate for more money, you want it in your salary, as opposed to a higher annual bonus or a signing bonus. Your base salary is most important, as it will often determine how much your next raise or bonus is (often calculated as a percentage of base salary), and may determine what your salary is in your next job, as it signals your market value. The "compound interest" on the base salary you negotiate today can be significant. You can use statements such as, *"Looking at the salary figure, I was anticipating something more in the range of X to Y,"* where X is your "fair and reasonable" number and Y is your "ideal" (see page 149).

Know when to stop speaking and start listening

Often it is nervousness that causes us to keep talking. Your points are best made simply and concisely. You may also find that the hiring manager is amenable to your requests and not much discussion is required around certain points. Give her ample time to respond to you. You also want to listen to what concerns she has that are not being stated, so that you can surface them and address them. For example, *"I sense that you are reluctant to increase the base salary because of the precedent that it might set…."*

Listen to their language

In negotiating, you are looking for openings in which to make your points heard. A hiring manager might say, "We don't *typically* give more than two weeks of vacation." Translation: "We sometimes *do* give more than two weeks of vacation." Words like "typically" or "usually" are cues that you should not cave or back down from your request, but gently nudge forward. In this case, you could respond with, *"I imagine there have been instances where more vacation time has been granted and I would like to discuss why this makes sense in my case."*

Frame your compensation requirements

Expressing the dollar figure as a percentage of an estimated budget, or comparing it to other professionals inside or outside the organization, can make your request seem more reasonable. For example, saying *"I know that at first glance this compensation figure seems high, but it actually represents only .05% of the annual budget I will be responsible for. In this context, it's a very small administrative cost."* By framing your request, you are also giving the hiring manager ammunition to sell your request internally, should she need to get additional approval.

Negotiation

STRATEGIES TO EMPLOY

Ask "What else might you be able to offer?"

Let's face it — employers don't want to spend money if they don't have to. Certain organizations are more flexible when it comes to negotiating, but at times there is a real limit to how high they can go. After coming to an impasse on the salary portion of the negotiation, or after you have communicated your requests with minimal accommodation from the hiring manager, ask the open-ended question: *"Given that you are not able to provide _____, what else might you be able to offer?"* The open-ended nature of this question forces them to play a card. Often hiring managers have been authorized to provide certain extras, (they usually have the most flexibility with signing bonuses), but they will not offer them unless asked or they can be persuaded to increase the signing bonus if one was offered. You don't know what these extras might be, so let the hiring manager present them to you. It may be something that you would not have thought to ask for.

Be patient

Recognize that you may have questions or requests that warrant further internal discussion at the organization, even if you are speaking to the decision maker. In this case, don't be afraid to wait a few more days until she can get back to you with some answers. You can say, *"I understand that you may need to speak with other people internally about this, so perhaps we can speak again in the next day or two after you've been able to discuss this issue."* In saying this, you are also signaling that you are not in a rush, which can give you additional negotiating power. Ideally, you don't want more than two additional iterations after receiving an offer, otherwise you (or she) will be signaling an inability to get things done.

Ask for what's fair

In making your requests, you can make statements such as, *"I want to come up with something that's fair for both of us."* By emphasizing fairness, you will again show that you are being reasonable and are not looking to gouge the organization. What makes this statement so effective is that it is very disarming — people can't argue with *fair*.

Don't be greedy

There is an expression, "Pigs get slaughtered." Know when you are asking for too much before you ask for it. It is also important to make sure your style and tone is not one of entitlement. Offers can be rescinded from candidates who conduct themselves poorly in this regard.

Leverage other offers

If you have other offers, let the hiring manager know the relevant elements to give her the opportunity and incentive to match or surpass these offers. We don't recommend using other offers as leverage and going down the negotiation path with an organization whose offer you know you will not accept, even if they do improve it. You will likely create ill-will, as it will be viewed as a waste of the hiring manager's time. If there is a chance you would accept the offer (even if they don't improve the offer), give it a go! You can say, *"Company B recently extended me an offer with a total compensation figure that was higher by 15%. I am still interested in this position and would like to know what flexibility you have to offer something comparable."*

Negotiation

STRATEGIES TO EMPLOY

Communicate how you value yourself

If the organization is not offering the compensation that you want, let the hiring manager know what your minimum acceptable compensation level is. This is not intended to be said in a threatening way, or be an ultimatum, but rather as a way to communicate to them what you need to feel valued and be properly motivated. Their flexibility, understanding, and willingness to listen to you will also be huge signals of what they are like to actually work for! You can say, *"I think what we both want is for me to start off on the right foot at the company. To feel good about my position and be properly motivated, I need to feel that the organization values my contribution. I don't think that I could feel good about working here if my compensation didn't reflect that."*

Define your "yes" package

This is a highly effective strategy. Before starting the negotiation conversation, you should always know the compensation and benefits package that you would be willing to say yes to on the spot. Proceed with your negotiations as you normally would. If you find that the hiring manager is reluctant to provide the additional salary, training budget, or some other element that is important to you, you can say something like, *"I think we are in agreement on most of these terms. If you could provide a package that includes $5,000 more in salary and an additional week of vacation, I am ready to accept right now and schedule my start date."* This is a *strong* leverage point for you as the candidate. There is *real* financial value to the employer to have this open position filled. Every day that goes by without the position filled is another day that someone else is doing the job in question, and another day that the hiring manager needs to spend hours away from her job to continue the recruiting process. Of course, the request still needs to be within reason and said in a tactful manner.

Know when to walk away

If the offer is truly underwhelming, or you feel taken advantage of, or not properly valued, or there is little trust or flexibility in the negotiations, these are all signals that it may be time to move on whether or not you have another offer. Your time may be better spent interviewing for that next great job.

Negotiation

OTHER IMPORTANT QUESTIONS TO ASK

In negotiating your compensation, here are some questions we recommend that you ask:

- What is the authorized salary range for this position?
- What salary grade is this position?
- What is the next higher salary grade and range?
- What have bonuses been for this position/in this department for the last few years?
- How quickly can I expect my base salary/total compensation to grow?
- How long does it typically take to get promoted from this position to the next level?

ACCEPTING AN OFFER

When accepting an offer, let the hiring manager know how excited you are. Set your start date and confirm follow-up logistics — will someone be sending you a written offer letter? Who will send it and when? Until you receive something in writing, it is a good idea to send the hiring manager an email reiterating your enthusiasm in joining the team and confirming all the details that you agreed upon (list the terms you agreed upon clearly and individually so there is no confusion). If HR has been involved, you may want to copy the HR representative on the email. Ask the hiring manager to confirm her understanding of the terms of the offer by replying to your email and to include the elements you highlighted in the offer letter. Once you receive her email reply, print it and save it in your files until you receive the written offer letter. Make sure the offer letter you receive actually reflects the terms outlined in your email. Don't assume it is all there.

DECLINING AN OFFER

If you have the luxury of deciding among multiple offers, you will invariably need to decline at least one offer, if not more. The goal is to do so graciously, letting the hiring manager know that you enjoyed getting to know her and you put real thought into your decision — and even that it was a tough decision, but you feel that another opportunity was better for you at this time in your career. Ideally, you want to leave the door open for future potential conversations (even if it is years down the road). We recommend that you decline person-to-person (likely by phone), as opposed to by email or voicemail, which is too passive. The decline of an offer might sound like, *"I am really flattered by your offer and I've put a lot of thought into it. While it's a wonderful opportunity, I feel that at this stage in my career, another opportunity that I received is better suited for me, so I unfortunately need to decline. I definitely enjoyed meeting you and the rest of the team — I have been quite impressed with the company and hope that our paths will cross again."*

Appendix
Additional Resources

Values List

FREQUENTLY MENTIONED VALUES

- **ACHIEVEMENT** — attaining goals, sense of accomplishment
- **ADVANCEMENT** — progress, promotion
- **ADVENTURE** — new and challenging experiences, risk
- **AESTHETICS** — making things more beautiful or having time to appreciate beauty
- **AFFILIATION** — a sense of belonging to a particular group
- **AFFLUENCE** — financial success, prosperity
- **AUTHORITY** — power to control events and activities of others
- **AUTONOMY** — personal control over time, sense of freedom, independence
- **BALANCE** — work, family, and leisure activities in the appropriate proportion
- **COLLABORATION** — cooperation, teamwork
- **COMPETENCE** — high degree of proficiency, knowledge, or expertise
- **COMPETITION** — striving to win, to be the best
- **CONTRIBUTION** — making a difference, improving society, helping others
- **CREATIVITY** — imaginative, inventive, original
- **ENJOYMENT** — fun, joy, and laughter
- **EXPERTISE** — mastery, expert skill, or knowledge
- **FAIRNESS** — justice, equality
- **FAMILY** — close relationships with family members
- **FINANCIAL REWARD** — abundance, wealth
- **FREEDOM** — ability to act or speak freely
- **FUN** — pleasure, enjoyment, good times
- **HEALTH** — physical and mental well-being
- **HELPING OTHERS** — providing care and support to others
- **INDIVIDUALITY** — free to define and express uniqueness
- **INFLUENCE** — impacting the opinions or decisions of others
- **INNER HARMONY** — at peace with self and others, tranquility

Values List

FREQUENTLY MENTIONED VALUES

- **INNOVATION** — contributing to new findings, products, or concepts
- **INTEGRITY** — honesty, sincerity, standing up for beliefs
- **INTELLECTUAL CHALLENGE** — analytical problem solving, cognitive engagement
- **KNOWLEDGE** — pursuit of understanding, skill, and expertise
- **LEADERSHIP** — the power and authority to manage operations, resources, and/or people
- **LEARNING** — introduction to new ideas, experiences, knowledge
- **LOYALTY** — commitment, dedication, dependability
- **MEMBERSHIP** — contributing to an organizational or group effort, sense of belonging
- **ORDER** — sense of stability, routine, predictability
- **PEOPLE CONTACT** — frequent interaction with others
- **PERSONAL DEVELOPMENT** — dedication to maximizing one's potential
- **PRESTIGE** — status, affiliation commands respect
- **RECOGNITION** — respect from others, acknowledgment
- **REFLECTION** — taking time out to think about the past, present, and future
- **RELATIONSHIPS** — developing or maintaining personal and professional relationships
- **RESPONSIBILITY** — accountability, reliability, ownership
- **SECURITY** — predictable income and future employment
- **SELF-RESPECT** — pride, self-esteem, sense of personal identity
- **SPIRITUALITY** — faith, strong spiritual and/or religious beliefs
- **STRUCTURE** — regular hours and predictable demands
- **TRADITION** — carrying on established rituals and practices
- **UNIQUENESS** — different or special in some way
- **VARIETY** — multiple activities, experiences, and tasks
- **WISDOM** — sound judgment based on knowledge, experience, and understanding

Action Verbs

Achieved	Designed	Integrated	Renegotiated
Administered	Developed	Interacted	Reorganized
Advised	Differentiated	Invested	Reported
Allocated	Directed	Investigated	Represented
Analyzed	Discovered	Launched	Researched
Anticipated	Distributed	Led	Resolved
Arranged	Diversified	Leveraged	Restructured
Assembled	Documented	Maintained	Retained
Assessed	Drafted	Managed	Revamped
Assisted	Drove	Mapped	Reviewed
Augmented	Earned	Maximized	Revitalized
Authored	Edited	Mentored	Saved
Authorized	Educated	Minimized	Secured
Balanced	Eliminated	Mitigated	Segmented
Budgeted	Enabled	Moderated	Selected
Built	Engineered	Monitored	Shaped
Captured	Enhanced	Negotiated	Shared
Chaired	Ensured	Obtained	Sold
Championed	Established	Opened	Solved
Coached	Evaluated	Optimized	Sourced
Collaborated	Evangelized	Orchestrated	Spearheaded
Collected	Exceeded	Organized	Started
Communicated	Executed	Originated	Streamlined
Completed	Expanded	Participated	Strengthened
Conceived	Facilitated	Partnered	Structured
Conducted	Financed	Performed	Supervised
Configured	Focused	Persuaded	Supported
Consolidated	Forecasted	Planned	Tackled
Consulted	Formulated	Positioned	Tailored
Contributed	Founded	Prepared	Targeted
Controlled	Funded	Presented	Tested
Convinced	Generated	Prioritized	Tracked
Coordinated	Grew	Produced	Trained
Counseled	Guided	Promoted	Transitioned
Crafted	Hired	Proposed	Upgraded
Created	Identified	Provided	Validated
Cultivated	Implemented	Recommended	Valued
Defined	Improved	Recruited	Volunteered
Delivered	Increased	Redefined	Won
Demonstrated	Initiated	Reduced	Worked
Deployed	Installed	Refined	Wrote

Mock Interview Evaluation Form

POISE

Had a firm handshake	○ Effective	○ Needs Work
Maintained good eye contact	○ Effective	○ Needs Work
Used hands appropriately while talking	○ Effective	○ Needs Work
Displayed confidence	○ Effective	○ Needs Work
Maintained appropriate facial expressions	○ Effective	○ Needs Work
Did not display nervous mannerisms	○ Effective	○ Needs Work

General Comments:

ARTICULATION

Did not interrupt	○ Effective	○ Needs Work
Listened to questions and comments	○ Effective	○ Needs Work
Spoke firmly and comfortably	○ Effective	○ Needs Work
Avoided using nonwords, e.g., *"um"*	○ Effective	○ Needs Work
Expressed self clearly	○ Effective	○ Needs Work
Did not ramble	○ Effective	○ Needs Work

General Comments:

MARKETING SELF

Discussed skills relevant to the position	○ Effective	○ Needs Work
Focused on relevant accomplishments	○ Effective	○ Needs Work
Used concrete examples to support statements	○ Effective	○ Needs Work
Expressed enthusiasm for the position	○ Effective	○ Needs Work
Stated career goals and related them to position	○ Effective	○ Needs Work
Indicated knowledge of and interest in the industry	○ Effective	○ Needs Work
Asked relevant and thoughtful questions	○ Effective	○ Needs Work
Closed by reiterating interest/commitment to position	○ Effective	○ Needs Work

General Comments:

Mock Interview Evaluation Form

POISE

Had a firm handshake	○ Effective ○ Needs Work
Maintained good eye contact	○ Effective ○ Needs Work
Used hands appropriately while talking	○ Effective ○ Needs Work
Displayed confidence	○ Effective ○ Needs Work
Maintained appropriate facial expressions	○ Effective ○ Needs Work
Did not display nervous mannerisms	○ Effective ○ Needs Work

General Comments:

ARTICULATION

Did not interrupt	○ Effective ○ Needs Work
Listened to questions and comments	○ Effective ○ Needs Work
Spoke firmly and comfortably	○ Effective ○ Needs Work
Avoided using nonwords, e.g., "um"	○ Effective ○ Needs Work
Expressed self clearly	○ Effective ○ Needs Work
Did not ramble	○ Effective ○ Needs Work

General Comments:

MARKETING SELF

Discussed skills relevant to the position	○ Effective ○ Needs Work
Focused on relevant accomplishments	○ Effective ○ Needs Work
Used concrete examples to support statements	○ Effective ○ Needs Work
Expressed enthusiasm for the position	○ Effective ○ Needs Work
Stated career goals and related them to position	○ Effective ○ Needs Work
Indicated knowledge of and interest in the industry	○ Effective ○ Needs Work
Asked relevant and thoughtful questions	○ Effective ○ Needs Work
Closed by reiterating interest/commitment to position	○ Effective ○ Needs Work

General Comments:

Mock Interview Evaluation Form

POISE

Had a firm handshake	○ Effective	○ Needs Work
Maintained good eye contact	○ Effective	○ Needs Work
Used hands appropriately while talking	○ Effective	○ Needs Work
Displayed confidence	○ Effective	○ Needs Work
Maintained appropriate facial expressions	○ Effective	○ Needs Work
Did not display nervous mannerisms	○ Effective	○ Needs Work

General Comments:

ARTICULATION

Did not interrupt	○ Effective	○ Needs Work
Listened to questions and comments	○ Effective	○ Needs Work
Spoke firmly and comfortably	○ Effective	○ Needs Work
Avoided using nonwords, e.g., "um"	○ Effective	○ Needs Work
Expressed self clearly	○ Effective	○ Needs Work
Did not ramble	○ Effective	○ Needs Work

General Comments:

MARKETING SELF

Discussed skills relevant to the position	○ Effective	○ Needs Work
Focused on relevant accomplishments	○ Effective	○ Needs Work
Used concrete examples to support statements	○ Effective	○ Needs Work
Expressed enthusiasm for the position	○ Effective	○ Needs Work
Stated career goals and related them to position	○ Effective	○ Needs Work
Indicated knowledge of and interest in the industry	○ Effective	○ Needs Work
Asked relevant and thoughtful questions	○ Effective	○ Needs Work
Closed by reiterating interest/commitment to position	○ Effective	○ Needs Work

General Comments:

Recommended Reading

CAREER EXPLORATION

Martha Beck, *Finding Your Own North Star*
How to navigate external influences and define your own interests and desires.

Po Bronson, *What Should I do with My Life?: The True Story of People Who Answered the Ultimate Question*
Tells the inspirational true stories of people who have found the most meaningful answers to that great question.

Mary Burton and Richard Wedemeyer, *In Transition: From the Harvard Business School Club of New York's Career Management Seminar*
Guidance drawn from the seminar that has helped more than a thousand Harvard MBAs advance their careers.

Timothy Butler, *Getting Unstuck*
How dead ends can illuminate and motivate positive life change. Butler is one of the creators of Career Leader® and Director of Career Development at Harvard Business School.

Julia Cameron, *The Artist's Way*
A supportive and insightful guide to awakening your creativity and taking your desires for an improved life seriously. A book for all thoughtful people, not just artists.

Herminia Ibarra, *Working Identity*
The best book on career transition for professionals, bar none, by a professor at INSEAD. Explores how career change is an iterative process of experimentation, shifting connections, and making sense of one's career path.

Robert Kaplan, *What You're Really Meant to Do: A Road Map for Reaching Your Unique Potential*
Kaplan shares a specific and actionable approach to defining your own success and reaching your potential. Provides an integrated plan for identifying and achieving your goals.

David Keirsey, *Please Understand Me*
A highly detailed description of the core temperaments related to the Myers Briggs Type Indicator.® Dense but very insightful about how the MBTI® shows up in careers and relationships.

Talane Miedaner, *Coach Yourself to Success*
A hundred and one coaching tips. Useful for anyone seeking to rebalance their life while moving forward.

Daniel Pink, *A Whole New Mind*
A convincing argument that the most satisfying and in-demand careers in the future will be those that combine left-brain and right-brain skills.

Srikumar S. Rao, *Are You Ready to Succeed?*
Based on a popular course at Columbia Business School on work/life satisfaction, a book that asserts that happiness and fulfillment are more likely to come from changes in your own perspectives and mental beliefs than from pure career achievement.

Paul Tieger and Barbara Barron, *Do What You Are*
Practical applications of the Myers Briggs Type Indicator® to career selection.

Recommended Reading

NETWORKING

Keith Ferrazzi, *Never Eat Alone*
The new classic on networking, based on the idea that all of our achievements are based on human relationships.

Devora Zack, *Networking for People Who Hate Networking: A Field Guide for Introverts, the Overwhelmed, and the Underconnected*
This book goes beyond the traditional approaches of small talk and constant contact to provide an approach for introverts that can be applied to all kinds of situations.

PERSONAL BRANDING

Dorie Clark, *Reinventing You: Define Your Brand, Imagine Your Future*
A mix of personal stories and examples from well-known personalities. Provides a step-by-step guide to assess your unique strengths and develop a compelling personal brand.

Reid Hoffman and Ben Casnocha, *The Start-Up of You: Adapt to the Future, Invest in Yourself, and Transform Your Career*
A blueprint for thriving in your job and building a career by applying the lessons of Silicon Valley's most innovative entrepreneurs.

Tom Peters, *The Brand You*
Thoughtful ideas about building your own brand.

INDEPENDENT CONSULTING

Marci Alboher, *One Person/Multiple Careers: How the Slash Effect Can Work for You*
Alboher, a lawyer turned writer, shows how "slash" careers can lead to personal and professional fulfillment.

Peter Block, *Flawless Consulting*
A useful book for any service professional.

Alan Weiss, *Million Dollar Consulting*
A classic guide to consulting that covers every aspect of developing a thriving consulting business.

SECOND ACT CAREERS

Marci Alboher, *The Encore Career Handbook: How to Make a Living and a Difference in the Second Half of Your Life*
A comprehensive, nuts-and-bolts guide to finding passion, purpose, and a paycheck in the second half of life.

Nancy Collamer, *Second-Act Careers: 50+ Ways to Profit from Your Passions During Semi-Retirement*
A career guide that rethinks the golden years, this handbook offers 50+ income models for creating flexible, fulfilling, and profitable work during the encore stage of one's career.

Richard Leider and Alan Webber, *Life Reimagined: Discovering Your New Life Possibilities*
A guide with simple steps, online exercises at AARP's LifeReimagined.org website, and real life examples to help readers discover talents and create a successful career path.

Recommended Reading

RE-ENTERING THE WORKFORCE

Catherine Clifford and Millie Froeb, *Your Career OnRamp*
Provides a 10-step plan with advice for women re-entering the workforce on everything from finding career inspiration to flexible career options.

Carol Fishman Cohen and Vivian Steir Rabin, *Back on the Career Track: A Guide for Stay-at-Home Moms Who Want to Return to Work*
Step-by-step exercises, inspiring stories, and resources in this look at when, how, and why women are returning to work after career breaks of a few months or many years.

Emma Gilbey Keller, *The Comeback*
Keller tells the stories of seven very different women from a variety of professions who sought to strike a balance between demanding careers and budding families.

Sylvia Ann Hewlett, *Off-Ramps and On-Ramps: Keeping Talented Women on the Road to Success*
Documents the successful efforts of a group of cutting-edge global companies to retain talented women and reintegrate them if they've already left.

NEGOTIATION

Mika Brzezinski, *Knowing Your Value*
An in-depth look at how women today achieve their deserved recognition and financial worth prompted by the author's own experience as co-host of Morning Joe.

Matthew J. DeLuca and Nanette F. DeLuca, *Perfect Phrases for Negotiating Salary & Job Offers*
Hundreds of ready-to-use phrases to help you get the best possible salary, perks, or promotion.

Brian Tracy, *Negotiation*
A concise guide that explains how to become a master negotiator, including key techniques and negotiating styles.

ONCE YOU HAVE THE JOB

George Bradt, Jayme Check, and Jorge Pedraza, *The New Leader's 100-Day Action Plan: How to Take Charge, Build Your Team, and Get Immediate Results*
Provides a comprehensive onboarding plan for the first 100 days in a new role including forms to help plan, approaches to motivate new team members, and tools for assessing the internal political culture.

Thomas Neff and James Citrin, *You're in Charge, Now What?: The 8 Point Plan*
An eight-point plan to show you how to lay the groundwork for long-term momentum and great performance and succeed in a new position.

Michael Watkins, *The First 90 Days, Updated and Expanded: Proven Strategies for Getting Up to Speed Faster and Smarter*
Watkins offers proven strategies for conquering the challenges of transitions—no matter where you are in your career. Watkins identifies the most common pitfalls and provides the tools and strategies to avoid them as well as advice on how to secure critical early wins.

OTHER

David Allen, *Getting Things Done*
Allen is a guru in the field of how to manage time and tasks for maximum effectiveness and happiness.

Useful Websites

ACCOUNTING AND FINANCE	AICPA: **www.aicpa.org** Association for Financial Professionals: **www.afponline.org** CFA Institute: **www.cfainstitute.org** Financial Executives Networking Group: **www.thefeng.org** FinancialJobs.com: **www.financialjobs.com** New York Institute of Finance: **www.nyif.com** Smart Pros: **www.accountingnet.com**
BIOTECH AND HEALTH CARE	Bio Online Career Center: **www.bio.com** HealthCareerWeb: **www.healthcareerweb.com** National Association of Healthcare Consultants: **www.healthcon.org** National Institutes of Health: **www.jobs.nih.gov**
BUSINESS AND JOB RESEARCH	Bizjournals.com: **www.bizjournals.com** Business Week: **www.businessweek.com** Careers in Business: **careers-in-business.jobsinthemoney.com** CEO Express: **www.ceoexpress.com** Corporate Information: **www.corporateinformation.com** Fortune: **www.fortune.com** glassdoor: **www.glassdoor.com** Hoovers Online: **www.hoovers.com** MBA Jungle: **www.mbajungle.com** Vault Insider Guide: **www.vault.com** WetFeet: **www.wetfeet.com** Yahoo Finance: **www.yahoo.com**
CAREER RE-ENTRY AND CHANGING CAREERS	Encore: **www.encore.org** Fullosophie: **www.fullosophie.com** irelaunch: **www.irelaunch.com** Life Reimagined[SM] for Work: **www.workreimagined.aarp.com** May Brooks: **www.maybrooks.com** Mom Corps: **www.momcorps.com** Pivotplanet **www.pivotplanet.com** (formerly **www.vocationvacations.com**) Your On Ramp: **www.youronramp.com**
COMPENSATION AND BENEFITS	Job Smart Salary Index Information: **www.jobsmart.org/tools/salary/index.htm** Payscale.com: **www.payscale.com** Salary.com: **www.salary.com** Salary Expert: **www.salaryexpert.com**
CONSULTING/ FLEXIBLE WORK	A-connect: **www.a-connect.com** Business Talent Group: **www.businesstalentgroup.com** Cambridge Consulting: **www.cambridgeconsultant.com** Consulting Base: **www.consultingbase.com** Contract Employment Weekly: **www.ceweekly.com** CPRi: **www.cpri.com** Crimson Consulting: **www.crimson-consulting.com** Dunhill Staffing: **www.dunhillstaff.com**

Useful Websites

CONSULTING/ FLEXIBLE WORK

Elance: **www.elance.com**
Flexible Resources: **www.flexibleresources.com**
Forshay: **www.forshay.com**
FreeAgent.com: **www.freeagent.com**
Guru.com: **www.guru.com**
HourlyNerd: **www.hourlynerd.com**
M2: **www.msquared.com**
Professional and Technical Consultants Association: **www.patca.com**

ENTREPRENEURSHIP

Forum for Women Entrepreneurs: **www.fwe.org**
Inc. Magazine: **www.inc.com**
Making It: **www.makingittv.com**
Small Business Development Centers: **www.sba.gov**
Entrepreneurs' Organization: **www.eonetwork.org**

ENGINEERING AND TECHNOLOGY

CIO Magazine: **www.cio.com**
Computer Jobs: **www.computerjobs.com**
DICE: **www.dice.com**
Engineering Jobs: **www.engineeringjobs.com**
Just Tech Jobs: **www.justtechjobs.com**
Society of Women Engineers: **www.swe.org**
Women in Technology: **www.witi.org**

ENVIRONMENTAL SUSTAINABILITY

Environmental Careers Organization: **www.eco.org**
Sustainable Business: **www.sustainablebusiness.com**

EXECUTIVE

6 Figure Jobs: **www.6figurejobs.com**
Career Journal (Wall Street Journal): **www.careerjournal.com**
Exec-U-Net: **www.execunet.com**
Five O'Clock Club: **www.fiveoclockclub.com**
Netshare.com: **www.netshare.com**
Vistage: **www.vistage.com**

GENERAL

Art of Networking: **www.quintcareers.com/networking.html**
Career Builder: **www.careerbuilder.com**
Career Exposure: **www.careerexposure.com**
Craig's List: **www.craigslist.org**
Indeed: **www.indeed.com**
LinkedIn: **www.linkedin.com**
MBA GlobalNet: **www.mbaglobalnet.com**
Monster: **www.monster.com**
Networking Associations and Societies: **www.job-hunt.org/associations.shtml**
True Careers: **www.truecareers.com**
Worktree: **www.worktree.com**
Yahoo Hot Jobs: **www.hotjobs.com**

Useful Websites

HUMAN RESOURCES
American Society for Training and Development: **www.astd.org**
National Human Resources Association: **www.humanresources.org**
Society of Human Resource Management: **www.shrm.org**
Workforce Online: **www.workforceonline.com**

IMMIGRATION RESOURCES
American Immigration Lawyers Association: **www.aila.org**
Association for International Practical Training: **www.aipt.org**
Fragomen: **www.fragomen.com**
H1 Base: **www.h1base.com**
H1-B Visa Jobs: **www.h1bvisajobs.com**
U.S. Citizenship and Immigration Services: **www.uscis.org**

INTERNATIONAL
Asia Net: **www.asia-net.com**
Bilingual Jobs.com: **www.bilingual-jobs.com**
Centre People: **www.centrepeople.com**
Chinese Information and Networking Association: **www.cina.org**
Euro Circle: **www.eurocircle.com**
Foreign MBA: **www.foreignmba.com**
Global Workplace: **www.global-workplace.com**
Going Global: **www.goingglobal.com**
Hire Diversity: **www.hirediversity.com**
Hobsons: **www.hobsons.com**
Idealist: **www.idealist.org**
Interaction: **www.interaction.org**
International Career Weekly: **www.internationaljobs.org**
International Development Jobs: **www.devnetjobs.org**
International Student: **www.internationalstudent.com**
Keizai Society: **www.keizai.org**
Latin MBA: **www.latinmba.com**
Latpro: **www.latpro.com**
MBA Enterprise Corps: **www.mbaec-cdc.org**
MBA Exchange: **www.mba-exchange.com**
One World.net: **www.oneworld.net**
Step Stone: **www.stepstone.com**
Wall Street Journal Asia: **www.careerjournalasia.com**
Wall Street Journal Europe: **www.careerjournaleurope.com**

MEDIA
Corporation for Public Broadcasting: **www.cpb.org**
Entertainment Careers: **www.entertainmentcareers.net**
TV Jobs: **www.tvjobs.com**

NON-PROFITS
ExecSearches: **www.execsearches.com**
Guidestar: **www.guidestar.com**
Idealist: **www.idealist.org**
NonprofitOyster.com: **www.nonprofitoyster.com**
OpportunityNOCS: **www.opportunitynocs.org**

Useful Websites

PHILANTHROPY
- Chronicle of Philanthropy: **www.philanthropy.com**
- Council on Foundations: **www.cof.org**
- Foundation Center: **www.fdncenter.org**

RECRUITERS
- Bluesteps: **www.bluesteps.com**
- Management Recruiters International: **www.mrinetwork.com**
- Christian and Timbers: **www.ctnet.com**
- Egon Zehnder: **www.zehnder.com**
- Future Step: **www.futurestep.com**
- Korn Ferry International: **www.kornferry.com**
- Heidrick & Struggles: **www.heidrick.com**
- Robert Half: **www.roberthalf.com**
- Recruiters Online: **www.recruitersonline.com**
- Russell Reynolds: **www.russellreynolds.com**
- Spencer Stuart: **www.spencerstuart.com**

SALES, MARKETING AND PUBLIC RELATIONS
- Adweek: **www.adweek.com**
- American Marketing Association: **www.ama.org**
- Careers in Marketing: **www.careers-in-marketing.com**
- Communications Roundtable: **www.roundtable.org**
- Direct Marketing Association: **www.the-dma.org**
- International Association of Business Communicators: **www.iabc.com**
- Marketing Executives Networking Group: **www.mengonline.com**
- Marketing Jobs: **www.marketingjobs.com**
- Marketing Research Association: **www.mra-net.org**
- Product Development and Management Association: **www.pdma.org**
- Sales Heads: **www.salesheads.com**

SOCIALLY RESPONSIBLE COMPANIES
- Business for Social Responsibility: **www.bsr.org**
- Social Venture Network Jobs Page: **www.svn.org**

TECHNOLOGY
- CrunchBase: **www.crunchbase.com**
- TechCrunch: **www.techcrunch.com**
- VentureLoop: **www.ventureloop.com**

VENTURE CAPITAL AND PRIVATE EQUITY
- Dow Jones Venture Capital: **www.venturecapital.dowjones.com**
- National Venture Capital Association: **www.nvca.org**
- Private Equity Central: **www.privateequitycentral.net**
- Private Equity Info: **www.privateequityinfo.com**
- Private Equity Search Digest: **www.jobsearchdigest.com/pesd**
- Venture Capital Task Force: **www.vctaskforce.com**
- Venture Reporter: **www.venturereporter.net**

About Next Step Partners

Next Step Partners is a widely recognized Career and Leadership Development firm. Through their work with MBA programs, corporations, and non-profits around the world, Next Step Partners has worked with thousands of professionals from all sectors — from the manager level to C–level executives. Whether it's working with a company to support their departing employees to find their next professional opportunity, or helping leaders to proactively take ownership of their careers within their current organization, Next Step Partners brings an intelligence, pragmatism, and unwavering professionalism that helps demystify the process of career development. The firm's partners and consultants are Executive Coaches with MBAs and other advanced degrees from Stanford, Yale, UC Berkeley, UCLA, and Wharton and have direct management experience in multiple functions and industries. They have frequently been quoted in the *New York Times*, the *Wall Street Journal* and *USA Today*, among other publications, on career and workplace issues.

For more information, visit **www.NextStepPartners.com**

Notes

Notes

Notes

Notes

Notes

Notes

Notes

Notes

Notes

Notes

Made in the USA
Columbia, SC
04 July 2019